Statistics with Rust

Second Edition

Explore rust programming and its powerful crates across data science, machine learning and NLP projects

Keiko Nakamura

Published by: GitforGits

Publisher: Sonal Dhandre

www.gitforgits.com

support@gitforgits.com

Printed in India

First Printing: October 2024

ISBN: 978-81-19177-97-4

Cover Design by: Kitten Publishing

Prologue

I set out to write "Statistics with Rust" with one clear vision: to merge the precision of statistical analysis with the performance and safety of Rust programming. This second edition builds upon the foundation of the first. The journey has been both challenging and rewarding, and I am pleased to present it. Rust has evolved remarkably over the past few years. It is now at version 1.72.0 and has brought enhanced features and a growing ecosystem of libraries. I was inspired to revisit the original content and incorporate the latest advancements in both statistics and Rust. My goal has always been to provide a hands-on experience, and this edition intensifies that focus with more practical programs and real-world examples.

This edition includes a deeper exploration of machine learning and natural language processing, which I am excited to share. I have added new chapters on nonlinear models, multivariate techniques, and text analysis. You will find implementations of algorithms like Support Vector Machines, Neural Networks, and Principal Component Analysis, all using Rust's powerful crates such as smartcore, linfa, and tch. These examples prove that Rust is the ideal tool for complex data analysis tasks.

Working with real datasets often presents challenges like handling large volumes of data and ensuring code efficiency. Rust is the ideal choice for tackling these issues thanks to its memory safety and performance. The book will show you how to leverage Rust's features to write robust and efficient code. You'll learn how to manipulate data using ndarray, perform statistical computations with ndarray-stats, and process text data with crates like regex and unicode-segmentation. Furthermore, I have made it a priority to include a strong focus on practical application. Each chapter includes code snippets and full programs that you can run and modify. You will have hands-on projects that reinforce the concepts discussed, whether you're building a regression model, performing hypothesis testing, or working on time series analysis.

I am especially proud of how this book bridges the gap between theory and practice. Statistics can feel abstract, but I've made them tangible and accessible by implementing the concepts in Rust. I explain not just the how, but also the why behind each method. This helps you develop a deeper understanding of both statistics and programming. Writing this book has been an incredible journey of learning and discovery for me. The Rust community is growing and innovating in ways that continually inspire me. This book will empower you to harness Rust's capabilities in your statistical work and open up new possibilities for analysis and application.

I'm grateful for the opportunity to share this passion with you. I'm confident you'll apply these tools and concepts in your own projects, and I'm certain we'll continue to make advancements together in the fields of statistics and Rust programming.

— Keiko Nakamura

Content

Preface

"Statistics with Rust, Second Edition" is designed to help you learn quickly, focusing on practical statistics using Rust scripts. The book is for readers who know the basics of statistics and machine learning. It gives quick explanations so you can try out concepts with hands-on coding.

The book uses the newest version of Rust, 1.72.0, to help users build and secure statistical and machine learning algorithms. Each chapter is full of useful programs and code examples that will walk you through tasks like data manipulation, statistical tests, regression analysis, building machine learning models, and natural language processing.

We've covered great Rust crates featured throughout, including:

- **ndarray and ndarray-linalg**: For efficient handling of multi-dimensional arrays and linear algebra operations.
- **ndarray-stats**: To perform statistical computations on arrays.
- **rand and rand_distr**: For generating random numbers and working with probability distributions.
- **smartcore**: A machine learning library used for implementing algorithms like decision trees and random forests.
- **linfa**: A toolkit providing implementations of Support Vector Machines and other algorithms.
- **tch**: Rust bindings for PyTorch, enabling the creation and training of neural networks.
- **finalfusion**: For working with word embeddings in natural language processing tasks.
- **rust-stemmers**: To perform stemming in text preprocessing.
- **regex**: For pattern matching and text manipulation.
- **unicode-segmentation**: To accurately tokenize Unicode strings.

This second edition brings all chapters up to date with the latest in stats and Rust programming. It focuses on how you can put these things to practical use, with a detailed look at advanced algorithms like PCA, SVM, neural networks, and ensemble methods. We've also included some natural language processing topics, such as text preprocessing, tokenization, and word embeddings.

The book also shows you how to combine Rust's performance and safety with statistical analysis, giving you the tools you need to do data analysis efficiently and reliably. The book's got lots of practical code and explanations that are easy to understand, which helps you learn the skills you need to get to grips with data using Rust.

GitforGits

Prerequisites

This book is perfect for every data user, including data scientist, NLP engineers, rust programmers, data engineers, data analysts and all those who are knowning simple basics of statistics and eager to use Rust programming for data science and machine learning projects.

Codes Usage

Are you in need of some helpful code examples to assist you in your programming and documentation? Look no further! Our book offers a wealth of supplemental material, including code examples and exercises.

Not only is this book here to aid you in getting your job done, but you have our permission to use the example code in your programs and documentation. However, please note that if you are reproducing a significant portion of the code, we do require you to contact us for permission.

But don't worry, using several chunks of code from this book in your program or answering a question by citing our book and quoting example code does not require permission. But if you do choose to give credit, an attribution typically includes the title, author, publisher, and ISBN. For example, "Statistics with Rust, Second Edition by Keiko Nakamura".

If you are unsure whether your intended use of the code examples falls under fair use or the permissions outlined above, please do not hesitate to reach out to us at support@gitforgits.com.

We are happy to assist and clarify any concerns.

Acknowledgement

I owe a tremendous debt of gratitude to GitforGits, for their unflagging enthusiasm and wise counsel throughout the entire process of writing this book. Their knowledge and careful editing helped make sure the piece was useful for people of all reading levels and comprehension skills. In addition, I'd like to thank everyone involved in the publishing process for their efforts in making this book a reality. Their efforts, from copyediting to advertising, made the project what it is today.

Finally, I'd like to express my gratitude to everyone who has shown me unconditional love and encouragement throughout my life. Their support was crucial to the completion of this book. I appreciate your help with this endeavour and your continued interest in my career.

CHAPTER 1: INTRODUCTION TO RUST FOR STATISTICIANS

Overview

In this first chapter, I will introduce you to the fascinating world of statistics and Rust programming. You will discover how Rust, a systems programming language known for its reliability and performance, can be used effectively for statistical analysis.

The chapter begins by assisting you in setting up your Rust development environment, ensuring that you have all of the necessary tools installed so you can begin coding immediately. You will learn about Rust's core features that make it ideal for statistical computing, such as its ownership model, memory safety guarantees, and concurrency capabilities. I will walk you through the fundamentals of Rust syntax, such as variables, data types, control flow, and functions, using examples that are directly relevant to statistical computations. We will look at important data structures such as arrays, vectors, and slices that are necessary for working with datasets. You will learn how to read data from files with the csv crate, allowing you to include real-world datasets in your Rust programs. In addition, we'll go over basic data manipulation techniques, so you can clean and prepare data for analysis.

By the end of this chapter, you will have written your first Rust programs for basic statistical operations. You will compute central tendency measures like mean and median, as well as dispersion measures like variance and standard deviation. These hands-on examples will help you improve both your Rust programming skills and your understanding of basic statistical concepts.

Why Rust for Data Analysis and Statistics?

In the dynamic world of data science and statistical computing, the tools we choose significantly influence the efficiency and scalability of our work. While languages like Python and R have been staples in the field due to their simplicity and rich ecosystems, Rust has emerged as a powerful alternative that brings unique advantages to statisticians and data analysts.

Rust is a systems programming language focused on safety, speed, and concurrency. Originally designed for system-level programming, Rust has evolved to address challenges in various domains, including data analysis and statistical computing. This chapter introduces Rust's potential in these fields, emphasizing why it is a compelling choice for statisticians and how it can enhance your data analysis projects.

High Performance

One of Rust's most significant strengths is its **high performance**. As a compiled language, Rust translates code directly into machine code without the overhead of a virtual machine or interpreter. This results in execution speeds comparable to or exceeding those of C and C++, making Rust ideal for computationally intensive tasks common in data analysis and statistics.

For example, when dealing with large datasets, implementing complex algorithms, or performing extensive simulations, Rust's performance can lead to substantial reductions in processing time.

This efficiency allows you to work with larger datasets and more complex models than might be feasible with interpreted languages.

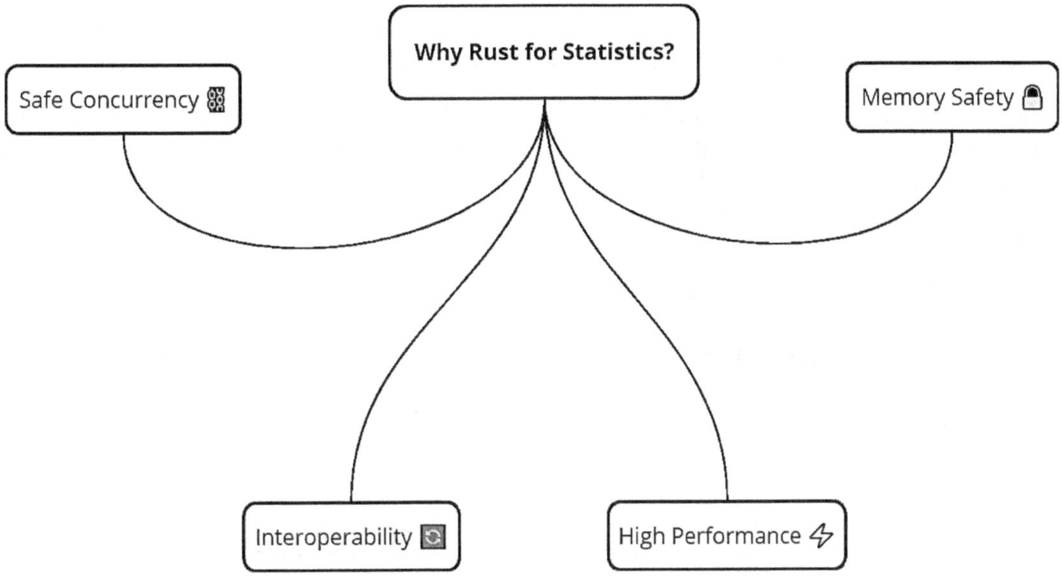

Fig 1.1 Features of Rust Programming

Memory Safety and Reliability

Memory safety is crucial when handling large amounts of data and intricate data structures. Common issues like null pointer dereferences, buffer overflows, and data races can lead to program crashes or subtle bugs that are difficult to diagnose.

Rust introduces a unique **ownership model** that enforces memory safety at compile time without requiring a garbage collector. This system ensures that each piece of data has a single owner, eliminating issues related to dangling pointers and data races in concurrent programs. The result is more robust and reliable code, giving you confidence in the correctness of your statistical analyses.

Safe Concurrency

Modern processors feature multiple cores, and leveraging concurrency is essential for maximizing performance. Rust's emphasis on safe concurrency allows you to write parallel code without fear of introducing hard-to-find bugs.

Rust's ownership and borrowing system ensures that data accessed by multiple threads is handled safely. This compile-time checking prevents common concurrency pitfalls such as race conditions and deadlocks. For data analysts, this means you can efficiently parallelize data processing tasks, significantly speeding up operations like data cleaning, transformation, and model training.

Interoperability and Ecosystem Integration

Rust's interoperability with other languages is another significant advantage. Through its Foreign Function Interface (FFI), Rust can seamlessly integrate with libraries written in C and C++. This capability allows you to leverage existing high-performance libraries for tasks like linear algebra, optimization, and machine learning, all while benefiting from Rust's safety guarantees.

Additionally, Rust's ecosystem is rapidly growing, with libraries tailored for data analysis and statistics. Crates (Rust's term for libraries) such as **ndarray** for multi-dimensional arrays, **Polars** for DataFrame operations, and **Plotters** for data visualization provide the tools necessary to perform complex analyses entirely in Rust.

WebAssembly and Cross-Platform Capabilities

Rust's support for **WebAssembly** (Wasm) opens up new avenues for deploying data analysis applications on the web. By compiling Rust code to Wasm, you can run computationally intensive tasks directly in web browsers, enabling interactive data visualizations and real-time analytics in web applications.

Moreover, Rust is inherently cross-platform. You can compile your programs for various operating systems, including Linux, macOS, and Windows, as well as for embedded systems. This flexibility ensures that your data analysis tools can be deployed wherever they are needed.

Modern Language for Modern Challenges

Rust incorporates modern programming language features that enhance developer productivity and code maintainability:

- **Strong Static Typing**: Rust's type system catches many errors at compile time, reducing runtime bugs and making code more predictable.
- **Pattern Matching**: Powerful pattern matching allows for more expressive and concise code, which is particularly useful in data manipulation and transformation tasks.
- **Expressive Syntax**: Rust's syntax is designed for clarity and conciseness, making it easier to read and write complex code.

By adopting Rust, you are embracing a language designed to meet the demands of today's data-intensive applications, providing a solid foundation for building efficient and reliable statistical tools.

Comparing Rust and Python for Statistics

Python has been the language of choice for many data scientists and statisticians due to its simplicity and extensive libraries like NumPy, pandas, and SciPy. However, as data grows in volume and complexity, Python's performance limitations become more apparent. We will look at a comparison between Rust and Python, highlighting how Rust addresses some of the shortcomings of Python in the statistical computing domain.

Performance Considerations

Python is an interpreted language, which introduces performance overhead. While libraries like NumPy mitigate this by utilizing optimized C code, Python can still be a bottleneck for compute-intensive tasks.

Rust's compiled nature means that code is optimized for the hardware it runs on, resulting in:

- **Faster Execution**: Ideal for simulations, numerical computations, and real-time data processing.
- **Lower Latency**: Essential for time-sensitive applications like high-frequency trading or live analytics.

Memory Management and Safety

Python relies on a garbage collector for memory management, which can introduce latency due to unpredictable pauses during execution. This can be problematic for applications requiring consistent performance.

Rust's ownership model provides deterministic memory management without a garbage collector, offering:

- **Predictable Performance**: No garbage collection pauses mean consistent execution times.
- **Memory Safety**: Compile-time checks prevent common bugs like null pointer dereferences and data races.
- **Resource Efficiency**: Fine-grained control over memory allocation allows for optimizing resource usage.

Concurrency and Parallelism

Python's Global Interpreter Lock (GIL) limits the execution of multiple threads, hindering multi-threaded performance. While workarounds exist, they often add complexity.

Rust excels in concurrency:

- **No GIL**: Rust allows true multi-threading without interpreter locks.
- **Safe Concurrency**: The compiler enforces rules that prevent data races.

- **Efficient Parallelism**: Libraries like **`Rayon`** simplify parallel computations over data collections.

Ecosystem and Libraries

Python's extensive ecosystem is one of its greatest strengths. However, Rust's ecosystem is rapidly growing, with many libraries reaching maturity.

Key Rust libraries for statistics and data analysis include:

- **`ndarray`**: N-dimensional array library similar to NumPy's ndarray.
- **`Polars`**: A fast DataFrame library inspired by pandas.
- **`Statrs`**: A statistics library providing distributions and statistical functions.
- **`Plotters`** and **`Plotly`**: Libraries for data visualization.

While Rust's ecosystem may not yet match Python's in breadth, its libraries are robust and continue to improve, offering a viable alternative for many data analysis tasks.

Development Experience

Python is known for its simplicity, making it accessible to beginners. Rust has a steeper learning curve due to its emphasis on safety and performance.

However, Rust provides:

- **Detailed Compiler Messages**: The compiler offers helpful error messages and suggestions.
- **Modern Tooling**: Cargo, Rust's build system and package manager, simplifies project and dependency management.
- **Strong Community Support**: An active community that is welcoming to newcomers.

Scalability and Maintainability

As projects grow, maintainability becomes critical. Python, while flexible, can become difficult to manage in large projects due to dynamic typing and potential runtime errors. Rust encourages writing clean, efficient code with enforced safety and correctness, making large codebases easier to maintain. Rust's strict compiler checks and explicitness help prevent bugs and make codebases more scalable.

Deployment and Portability

Deploying Python applications can be challenging due to dependencies and environment configurations.

Rust offers:

- **Static Binaries**: Compiled executables with no external dependencies simplify deployment.
- **Cross-Compilation**: Compile code for different platforms from a single system.
- **Embedded Systems Support**: Rust is suitable for embedded development, expanding its applicability.

Although Python remains a popular and powerful language for data analysis and statistics, Rust offers several advantages that make it a compelling alternative. Rust's high performance, support for concurrency, and its growing ecosystem position it as a strong contender for future data analysis needs.

Setting up Rust on Linux

To start using Rust for statistical computing, you will need to set up your development environment on Linux Ubuntu. Rust's installation process is straightforward, and its tooling makes it easy to manage your toolchain and dependencies. The recommended way to install Rust is through **Rustup**, a toolchain installer that manages Rust versions and associated tools.

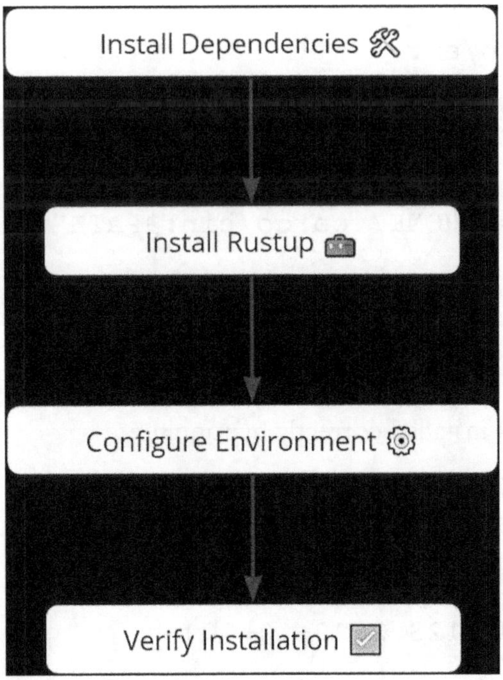

Fig 1.2 Step-by-step Rust Installation

Install Required Dependencies

Before installing Rustup, ensure that your system has the necessary build tools. Then, open the terminal and run:

```
sudo apt update
sudo apt install build-essential curl
```

This command installs essential compilation tools and **curl**, which is used to download Rustup.

Install Rustup

Next, run the following command in your terminal:

```
curl --proto '=https' --tlsv1.2 -sSf https://sh.rustup.rs | sh
```

You will be prompted to choose the installation type. **Press 1** to proceed with the default installation. The default installation includes the latest stable version of Rust.

Configure Environment

After installation, Rustup will suggest adding Rust to your system **PATH**. You can do this by running:

```
source $HOME/.cargo/env
```

To make this change permanent, add the following line to your shell profile file (e.g., **~/.bashrc**, **~/.profile**, or **~/.zshrc**):

```
echo 'export PATH="$HOME/.cargo/bin:$PATH"' >> ~/.bashrc
```

Then, reload your shell configuration:

```
source ~/.bashrc
```

Now, check whether Rust is installed correctly by running:

```
rustc --version
```

You should see output similar to:

```
rustc 1.73.0 (abcdef123 2023-10-10)
```

This confirms that the Rust compiler is installed and ready to use. Rust is actively developed, with new stable releases every six weeks. So, to update your Rust installation, use Rustup:

```
rustup update
```

This command updates Rust and its associated tools to the latest versions.

Essential Rust Libraries for Statistics

To perform statistical analysis and data manipulation, you will rely on several key libraries (crates). Below are some of the most important ones, which have matured significantly and offer robust functionality for statisticians.

'Ndarray' for N-Dimensional Arrays

Ndarray provides support for N-dimensional arrays and matrix operations, similar to NumPy's ndarray in Python. The github repo is accessible at following url:

https://github.com/rust-ndarray/ndarray

Some of the key attributes of ndarray:

- Support for multi-dimensional arrays with shape and strides.
- Efficient operations, including element-wise, broadcasting, and linear algebra
- operations.
- Various array manipulation methods, such as slicing, stacking, reshaping, and
- concatenation.
- Interoperability with BLAS and LAPACK libraries for high-performance linear algebra computations.

Given below is a quick example of ndarray:

```
use ndarray::Array2;
fn main() {
    // Create a 2x2 array filled with 1.0
    let a = Array2::from_elem((2, 2), 1.0);
    println!("Array:\n{:?}", a);
}
```

'Polars' for DataFrames

Polars is a fast DataFrame library for Rust, offering functionality similar to pandas. The github repo is accessible at following url:

https://github.com/pola-rs/polars

Following are the key attributes of polars:

- **DataFrame Operations**: GroupBy, Join, Pivot, and more.
- **Lazy Evaluation**: Optimize query execution plans for performance.
- **Multi-Threaded**: Utilize all CPU cores for data processing.
- **Interoperability**: Read from and write to CSV, Parquet, and JSON files.

Given below is a quick example of polars:

```
use polars::prelude::*;
fn main() -> Result<()> {
    // Read a CSV file into a DataFrame
    let df = CsvReader::from_path("data.csv")?
        .infer_schema(None)
        .has_header(true)
        .finish()?;
    println!("DataFrame Head:\n{}", df.head(Some(5)));
    Ok(())
}
```

'Statrs' for Statistical Computations

Statrs is a statistics library providing distributions and statistical functions. The github repo is accessible at following url:

https://github.com/boxtown/statrs

Some of the features of statrs:

- Support for common probability distributions, such as Normal, Poisson, Bernoulli,
- and more.
- Various descriptive statistics functions, like mean, variance, standard deviation,

- skewness, and kurtosis.
- Hypothesis testing functions, such as t-test, chi-square test, and F-test.
- Correlation and regression analysis functions.

Given below is a quick example of statrs:

```
use statrs::distribution::{Normal, ContinuousCDF};
fn main() {
    let normal = Normal::new(0.0, 1.0).unwrap();
    let probability = normal.cdf(1.96);
    println!("P(Z <= 1.96) = {}", probability);
}
```

'Plotters' for Data Visualization

Plotters is a drawing library designed for data visualization, supporting both static and interactive outputs. The github repo is accessible at following url:

https://github.com/plotters-rs/plotters

Some of the key attributes of plotters:

- **Multiple Backends**: Render to bitmap, SVG, PDF, or real-time GUI windows.
- **Flexible API**: Create complex charts like line plots, histograms, and heatmaps.
- **Customizable**: Fine-tune every aspect of your plots.

Given below is a quick example of plotters:

```
use plotters::prelude::*;
fn main() -> Result<(), Box<dyn std::error::Error>> {
    let root = BitMapBackend::new("output.png", (640,
480)).into_drawing_area();
    root.fill(&WHITE)?;
    let mut chart = ChartBuilder::on(&root)
        .caption("Sample Plot", ("sans-serif",
50).into_font())
        .build_cartesian_2d(0.0..10.0, 0.0..100.0)?;
```

```
    chart.draw_series(LineSeries::new(
        (0..100).map(|x| x as f64 / 10.0).map(|x| (x, x * x)),
        &RED,
    ))?;
    Ok(())
}
```

Setting up Statistical Project

Let's walk through setting up a new Rust project on Linux that utilizes the previously discussed libraries.

Create a New Cargo Project

Open your terminal and run:

```
cargo new my_statistical_project
cd my_statistical_project
```

This creates a new Rust project with the following structure:

```
my_statistical_project/
├── Cargo.toml
└── src
    └── main.rs
```

Add Dependencies

Edit **Cargo.toml** to include the libraries:

```
[dependencies]
ndarray = "0.15"
polars = { version = "0.32", features = ["lazy", "csv-file"] }
statrs = "0.14"
plotters = { version = "0.3", features = ["bitmap"] }
```

Here, ensure you have the latest versions in your development environment by checking crates.io or the library repositories.

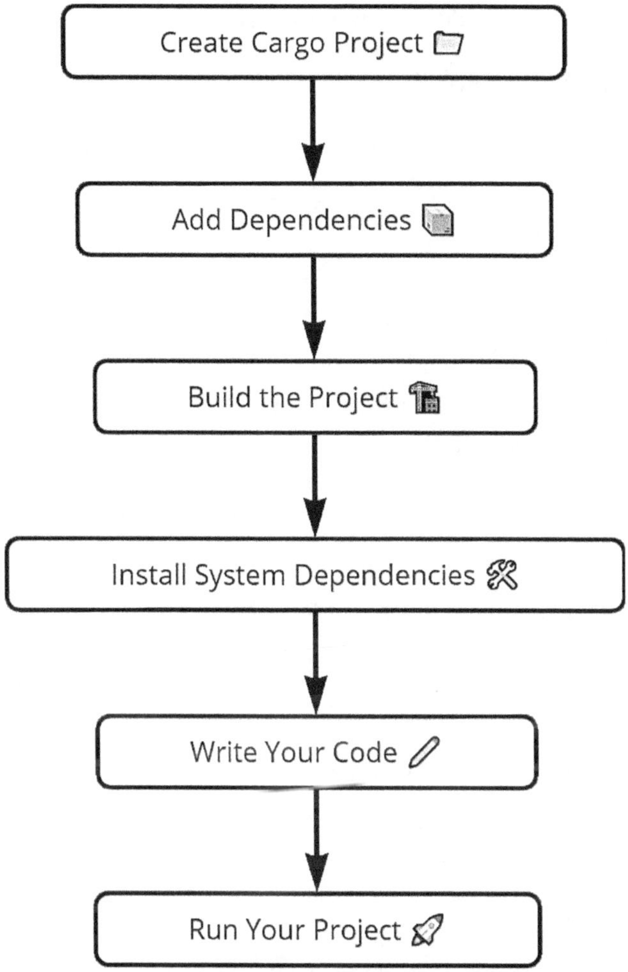

Fig 1.3 Setting up Statistical Project

Build Project

Run the following:

```
cargo build
```

Cargo will download and compile the dependencies.

Install System Dependencies

Some libraries, like **Polars**, may require additional system dependencies. Install them using:

```
sudo apt install pkg-config libssl-dev
```

For **Plotters**, if you plan to render plots as images, ensure you have the necessary fonts:

```
sudo apt install fonts-dejavu
```

Write Code

To write, edit the src/main.rs:

```
use ndarray::Array2;
use polars::prelude::*;
use statrs::distribution::{Normal, ContinuousCDF};
use plotters::prelude::*;
fn main() -> Result<(), Box<dyn std::error::Error>> {
    // Ndarray example
    let a = Array2::from_elem((2, 2), 1.0);
    println!("Array:\n{:?}", a);
    // Polars example
    let df = CsvReader::from_path("data.csv")?
        .infer_schema(None)
        .has_header(true)
        .finish()?;
    println!("DataFrame Head:\n{}", df.head(Some(5)));
    // Statrs example
    let normal = Normal::new(0.0, 1.0)?;
    let probability = normal.cdf(1.96);
    println!("P(Z <= 1.96) = {}", probability);
    // Plotters example
    let root = BitMapBackend::new("output.png", (640,
480)).into_drawing_area();
    root.fill(&WHITE)?;
```

```
    let mut chart = ChartBuilder::on(&root)
        .caption("Sample Plot", ("sans-serif",
50).into_font())
        .build_cartesian_2d(0.0..10.0, 0.0..100.0)?;
    chart.draw_series(LineSeries::new(
        (0..100).map(|x| x as f64).map(|x| (x, x.sqrt())),
        &RED,
    ))?;
    Ok(())
}
```

Now here, you need to check if you have a **data.csv** file in your project directory, otherwise you need to adjust the code to match your data source.

Run Project

Execute the following:

```
cargo run
```

This command compiles and runs your code, producing output in the terminal and generating a plot image (**output.png**).

Understanding Rust's Ownership Model

Before proceeding further, it's very much of importance to grasp Rust's ownership model, which underpins its memory safety guarantees. Knowing the concept of ownership, borrowing, and lifetimes within Rust helps writing efficient and error-free codes much easier than ever.

Ownership Rules

- **Each Value Has a Single Owner**: When you assign a value to a variable, that variable becomes its owner.
- **Values Are Dropped When Their Owner Goes Out of Scope**: Rust automatically deallocates memory when the owner goes out of scope.
- **Transfer of Ownership (Move Semantics)**: Assigning a value to another variable moves ownership.

Given below is a quick example of ownership rules:

```
fn main() {
    let s1 = String::from("hello");
    let s2 = s1; // s1 is moved to s2
    // println!("{}", s1); // Error: s1 has been moved
    println!("{}", s2);
}
```

Borrowing

Borrowing allows you to reference data without taking ownership.

- **Immutable Borrowing** (**`&T`**): Multiple immutable references are allowed.
- **Mutable Borrowing** (**`&mut T`**): Only one mutable reference is allowed at a time.

Given below is a quick example of borrowing:

```
fn main() {
    let mut data = vec![1, 2, 3];
    let ref1 = &data;
    let ref2 = &data;
    // let ref3 = &mut data; // Error: cannot borrow `data` as
mutable because it is also borrowed as immutable
    println!("{:?} {:?}", ref1, ref2);
}
```

Lifetimes

Lifetimes ensure that references are valid for as long as they are used. Given below is a quick example of lifetimes:

```
fn main() {
    let r;
    {
        let x = 5;
```

```
        r = &x;
        // x goes out of scope here
    }
    // println!("{}", r); // Error: `x` does not live long
enough
}
```

It is of the utmost importance to gain an understanding of these concepts if one is to work proficiently with Rust, particularly when dealing with complex data structures that are common in the field of statistical computing.

Summary

This chapter has given you an introduction to the potent mix of statistics and Rust programming. You configured your Rust development environment and became acquainted with the language's syntax and core concepts, such as variables, data types, ownership, and borrowing. You learned about Rust's data structures, such as arrays and vectors for managing statistical data. You learned to use the csv crate to read data from CSV files. You prepared datasets for analysis by using basic data manipulation techniques to ensure clean and well-structured.

You wrote Rust programs to perform basic statistical calculations like mean and median. You also calculated measures of dispersion, such as variance and standard deviation, which helped you better understand how these statistics describe data distributions. You closed the gap between theory and practice, gaining confidence in using Rust for statistical analysis. With the skills you've gained in this chapter, you can move on to more advanced topics in statistics and machine learning algorithms. You have made an important first step toward your goal, laying the groundwork for a thorough examination of data analysis with Rust in the subsequent chapters.

CHAPTER 2: DATA HANDLING AND PREPROCESSING

Introduction

In this chapter, you will learn about descriptive statistics and how to visualize data. The first thing that we are going to do is studying various measures of central tendency and dispersion, such as the mean, median, mode, variance, and standard deviation. Your understanding will be strengthened through the use of practical coding exercises as you learn how to calculate these statistics by utilizing Rust's ndarray and ndarray-stats crates.

In addition to introducing data analysis, the chapter goes over data visualization techniques. With the help of Rust's plotters crate, you will learn how to generate graphical representations such as scatter plots, box plots, and histograms. You will be able to effectively discover patterns and insights by the time you reach the end of this chapter.

Understanding Data Preprocessing

Why Preprocess Data?

Data preprocessing is a critical step because:

- **Improves Data Quality**: Cleans errors and inconsistencies, leading to more accurate results.
- **Enhances Performance**: Reduces computational load by eliminating irrelevant or redundant data.
- **Facilitates Analysis**: Transforms data into a suitable format for analysis or modeling.
- **Mitigates Bias**: Addresses issues like missing values and outliers that could skew results.

Process of Data Handling and Preprocessing

Conceptually, data handling and preprocessing encompass several tasks, including:

- Data collection: Acquiring and gathering data from various sources, such as databases, APIs, sensors, or user-generated content.
- Data cleaning: Identifying and correcting errors, inconsistencies, and inaccuracies in the data. This may involve handling missing values, removing duplicates, correcting typos, or standardizing formats.
- Data transformation: Converting data into a suitable format or structure for subsequent analysis. Examples of data transformations include normalization, scaling, encoding categorical variables, and aggregating data at different levels of granularity.

- Data integration: Combining data from multiple sources and ensuring consistency and compatibility among different datasets. This may require resolving conflicts in data formats, units, or variable names.
- Feature engineering: Deriving new features or variables from the raw data that can improve the performance of machine learning algorithms or provide additional insights during analysis.
- Data splitting: Dividing data into training, validation, and test sets for machine learning algorithms to prevent overfitting and evaluate model performance accurately.

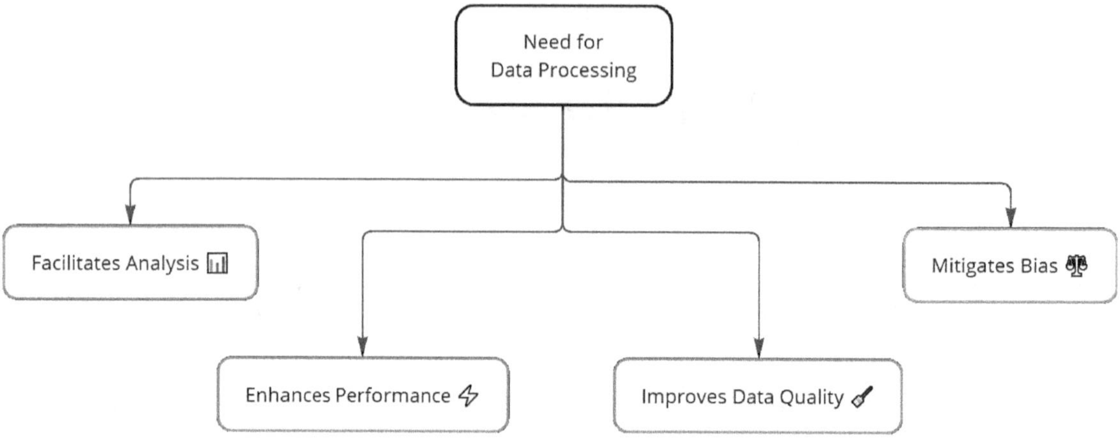

Fig 2.1 Purpose of Data Processing

Neglecting data preprocessing can lead to incorrect conclusions, unreliable models, and wasted resources.

In further topics of this chapter, we'll cover these steps using a real-world dataset.

Sample Dataset Overview

We will work with a dataset containing salary information for various roles in the data science field. This dataset is publicly available and contains rich information suitable for practicing data handling and preprocessing.

Dataset URL:

https://raw.githubusercontent.com/kittenpub/database-repository/main/ds_salaries.csv

The above dataset consists of 11 columns:

- **work_year**: The year the salary was paid.

- **experience_level**: The experience level in the job during the year.
- **employment_type**: The type of employment for the role.
- **job_title**: The role worked during the year.
- **salary**: The total gross salary amount paid.
- **salary_currency**: The currency of the salary paid.
- **salary_in_usd**: The salary in USD.
- **employee_residence**: Employee's primary country of residence during the work year.
- **remote_ratio**: The overall amount of work done remotely.
- **company_location**: The country of the employer's main office.
- **company_size**: The median number of people that worked for the company during the year.

It is of the utmost importance to gain an understanding of the structure of the dataset before embarking upon the processes of data handling and pre-processing.

Loading and Parsing Data

To work with the dataset, we'll need to load it into our Rust program and parse it into a usable format.

Setting up Project

Create a new Rust project for our data preprocessing tasks:

```
cargo new data_preprocessing
cd data_preprocessing
```

This above command initializes a new Rust project with a **Cargo.toml** file and a **src** directory containing **main.rs**.

Adding Dependencies

We will use the following crates:

- **`csv`**: For reading and writing CSV files.
- **`reqwest`**: For making HTTP requests to fetch data.

- **serde**: For serializing and deserializing data structures.
- **rand**: For random number generation (used later for data splitting).

Then, update your **Cargo.toml**:

```
[dependencies]
csv = "1.1"
reqwest = { version = "0.11", features = ["blocking"] }
serde = { version = "1.0", features = ["derive"] }
rand = "0.8"
```

Defining Data Structure

We will define a Rust struct that maps to the CSV columns:

```
use serde::Deserialize;
#[derive(Debug, Deserialize)]
struct SalaryRecord {
    work_year: u16,
    experience_level: String,
    employment_type: String,
    job_title: String,
    salary: f64,
    salary_currency: String,
    salary_in_usd: f64,
    employee_residence: String,
    remote_ratio: u8,
    company_location: String,
    company_size: String,
}
```

In the above script,

- The **#[derive(Debug, Deserialize)]** attribute automatically implements the **Debug** and **Deserialize** traits for **SalaryRecord**.
- Each field corresponds to a column in the CSV file.
- Data types are chosen based on the nature of the data.

Fetching Dataset

We will fetch the dataset using the **reqwest** crate:

```
use reqwest::blocking::get;
use std::error::Error;
fn fetch_dataset(url: &str) -> Result<String, Box<dyn Error>>
{
    let response = get(url)?.text()?;
    Ok(response)
}
```

Here,

- The function **fetch_dataset** sends a GET request to the URL and returns the response body as a **String**.
- The **?** operator propagates errors, making error handling concise.

Loading and Parsing CSV Data

We will parse the CSV data using the **csv** crate:

```
use csv::ReaderBuilder;
fn load_dataset(csv_data: &str) -> Result<Vec<SalaryRecord>,
Box<dyn Error>> {
    let mut reader = ReaderBuilder::new()
        .has_headers(true)
        .from_reader(csv_data.as_bytes());
    let mut records = Vec::new();
    for result in reader.deserialize() {
        let record: SalaryRecord = result?;
```

```
        records.push(record);
    }
    Ok(records)
}
```

Here, we use **ReaderBuilder** to configure the CSV reader. The **deserialize** method converts each CSV record into a **SalaryRecord** instance.

Main Function

Integrate the functions into **main**:

```
fn main() -> Result<(), Box<dyn Error>> {
    let url =
"https://raw.githubusercontent.com/kittenpub/database-
repository/main/ds_salaries.csv";
    let csv_data = fetch_dataset(url)?;
    let dataset = load_dataset(&csv_data)?;
    println!("Loaded {} records", dataset.len());
    Ok(())
}
```

By doing this,

- We fetch the CSV data from the URL.
- We load and parse the dataset.
- We print the number of records loaded.

Finally, run the program to ensure everything works:

```
cargo run
```

You should see an output like:

```
Loaded 500 records
```

This indicates that the dataset has been successfully loaded.

Exploring Dataset

Before diving into preprocessing, it's helpful to explore the dataset to understand its contents and identify potential issues.

Viewing Sample Records

Let us print a few sample records from the dataset:

```
for record in dataset.iter().take(5) {
    println!("{:?}", record);
}
```

Here, we use **iter().take(5)** to iterate over the first five records. The **println!("{:?}", record);** prints the record using the **Debug** trait.

Counting Unique Job Titles

Now, let us try to determine the number of unique job titles:

```
use std::collections::HashSet;

let unique_job_titles: HashSet<_> = dataset.iter().map(|r|
&r.job_title).collect();

println!("Number of unique job titles: {}",
unique_job_titles.len());
```

We can use **HashSet** that collects unique job titles And then, **map(|r| &r.job_title)** to extract the job title from each record.

Calculating Average Salary

Similarly, let us try to compute the average salary in USD:

```
let average_salary = dataset.iter().map(|r|
r.salary_in_usd).sum::<f64>() / dataset.len() as f64;

println!("Average salary in USD: {:.2}", average_salary);
```

Here, we sum all **salary_in_usd** values and divide by the number of records. The **{:.2}** formats the output to two decimal places.

Data Cleaning

Data cleaning involves handling missing values, correcting errors, and removing duplicates.

Handling Missing Values

Check for missing salaries:

```
let missing_salaries = dataset.iter().filter(|r|
r.salary_in_usd.is_nan()).count();
println!("Number of records with missing salary: {}",
missing_salaries);
```

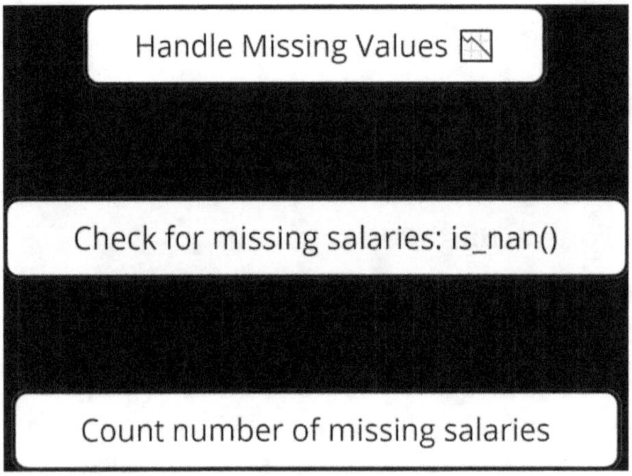

Fig 2.2 Managing Missing Values

In the above script,

- **is_nan()** checks if a value is "Not a Number," indicating missing data.
- We count how many records have missing salaries.

Now, remembe that in this dataset, there may be no missing values, but it's good practice to check. Also, the missing values can be filled in with default values based on the remaining data set. The most commonly employed imputation methods include:

- Mean: Replace missing values with the mean of the available data for the feature.
- Median: Replace missing values with the median of the available data for the feature.
- Mode: Replace missing values with the mode (most frequent value) of the available data for the feature.

- k-Nearest Neighbors: Fill in missing values based on the values of their k-nearest neighbors in the feature space.
- Regression: Predict missing values using a regression model trained on the available data.

Removing Duplicates

The duplicates are always harmful, primarily resulting to skew the analysis. The best way to remove them can be based on unique combinations of certain fields.

For example:

```
let mut seen = HashSet::new();
let mut unique_dataset = Vec::new();
for record in dataset {
    let key = (record.work_year, record.job_title.clone(),
record.company_location.clone());
    if seen.insert(key) {
        unique_dataset.push(record);
    }
}
println!("Dataset size after removing duplicates: {}",
unique_dataset.len());
```

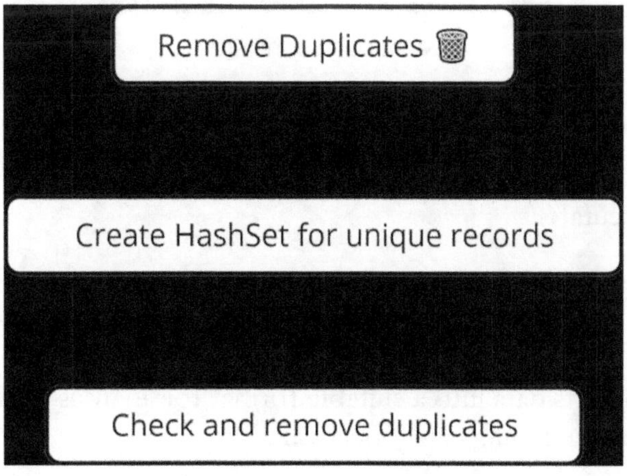

Fig 2.3 Removal of Duplicates

In the above script,

- We create a **HashSet** called **seen** to track unique records.
- If a record's key is not in **seen**, we add it to **unique_dataset**.

Correcting Inconsistencies

Standardize text fields, such as **experience_level**, to ensure consistency:

```
for record in &mut unique_dataset {
    record.experience_level =
record.experience_level.to_uppercase();
}
let experience_levels: HashSet<_> =
unique_dataset.iter().map(|r| &r.experience_level).collect();
println!("Experience levels: {:?}", experience_levels);
```

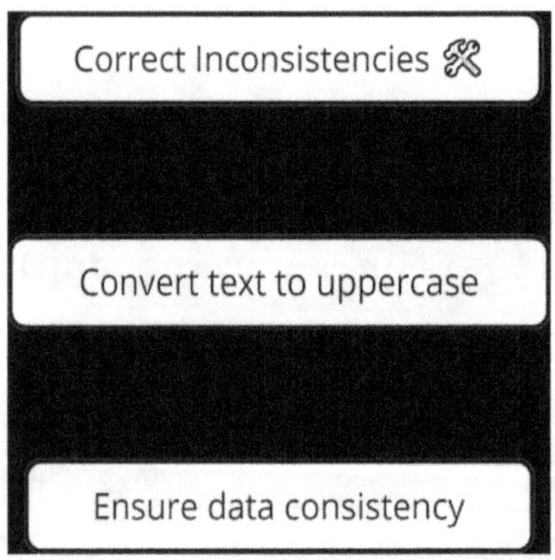

Fig 2.4 Correcting Data Inconsistency

In this, we converted all the **experience_level** values to uppercase. This ensures consistency, making analysis more accurate.

Data Transformation

Data transformation converts data into a suitable format for analysis. This is done primarily with numerical data scaling and encoding categorical variables.

Scaling Numerical Data

Scaling ensures that features contribute equally to analysis. Here, we will standardize the **salary_in_usd** using Z-score normalization:

```
fn calculate_mean(data: &[f64]) -> f64 {
    data.iter().sum::<f64>() / data.len() as f64
}
fn calculate_std_dev(data: &[f64], mean: f64) -> f64 {
    let variance = data.iter().map(|&x| (x - mean).powi(2)).sum::<f64>() / data.len() as f64;
    variance.sqrt()
}
let salaries: Vec<f64> = unique_dataset.iter().map(|r| r.salary_in_usd).collect();
let mean_salary = calculate_mean(&salaries);
let std_dev_salary = calculate_std_dev(&salaries, mean_salary);
let standardized_salaries: Vec<f64> = salaries.iter().map(|&s| (s - mean_salary) / std_dev_salary).collect();
println!("Standardized salaries (first 5): {:?}", &standardized_salaries[..5]);
```

In the above, we calculated the mean and standard deviation of salaries. Here, each salary is standardized by subtracting the mean and dividing by the standard deviation.

Encoding Categorical Variables

Next, we will convert categorical variables into numerical format using One-Hot Encoding for Job Titles:

```
use std::collections::HashMap;
fn one_hot_encode(values: &[String]) -> (Vec<Vec<u8>>, HashMap<String, usize>) {
    let unique_values: Vec<String> = values.iter().cloned().collect::<HashSet<_>>().into_iter().collect();
    let mut value_to_index = HashMap::new();
```

```
    for (i, value) in unique_values.iter().enumerate() {
        value_to_index.insert(value.clone(), i);
    }
    let encoded_values = values.iter().map(|value| {
        let mut vector = vec![0u8; unique_values.len()];
        if let Some(&index) = value_to_index.get(value) {
            vector[index] = 1;
        }
        vector
    }).collect();
    (encoded_values, value_to_index)
}
let job_titles: Vec<String> = unique_dataset.iter().map(|r|
r.job_title.clone()).collect();
let (encoded_job_titles, job_title_mapping) =
one_hot_encode(&job_titles);
println!("One-hot encoded job titles (first record): {:?}",
&encoded_job_titles[0]);
```

Here, we created a mapping from job titles to indices. And, each job title is represented as a binary vector where only one element is **1**.

Now, we will do Label Encoding for Experience Levels as below:

```
let experience_levels: Vec<String> =
unique_dataset.iter().map(|r|
r.experience_level.clone()).collect();
let unique_experience_levels: Vec<String> =
experience_levels.iter().cloned().collect::<HashSet<_>>().into
_iter().collect();
let mut experience_level_mapping = HashMap::new();
for (i, level) in unique_experience_levels.iter().enumerate()
{
    experience_level_mapping.insert(level.clone(), i);
```

```
}
let encoded_experience_levels: Vec<usize> =
experience_levels.iter().map(|level|
experience_level_mapping[level]).collect();
println!("Encoded experience levels (first 5): {:?}",
&encoded_experience_levels[..5]);
```

In this, each experience level is assigned a unique integer. This numerical representation can be used in models that require numerical input.

Feature Engineering

Feature engineering aims to create new, meaningful features from the existing data to improve the performance of machine learning models or provide additional insights. Some of the techniques that contribute to feature engineering prcoess includes:

- Multiplying or dividing two or more features to capture their combined effect on the target variable.
- Generating higher-order terms of the original features to capture non-linear relationships between variables.
- Applying expert knowledge from the problem domain to derive new, meaningful features (e.g., calculating the age of a customer from their birth date or extracting keywords from text data).

To understand it better, we create a binary feature indicating whether a role is fully remote as demonstrated below:

```
let remote_work_indicator: Vec<u8> =
unique_dataset.iter().map(|r| if r.remote_ratio == 100 { 1 }
else { 0 }).collect();
println!("Remote work indicator (first 5): {:?}",
&remote_work_indicator[..5]);
```

Next, we assign numerical scores to company sizes based on predefined categories.

```
fn company_size_score(size: &str) -> u8 {
    match size {
        "S" => 1, // Small
        "M" => 2, // Medium
```

```
        "L" => 3, // Large
        _ => 0,
    }
}
let company_size_scores: Vec<u8> =
unique_dataset.iter().map(|r|
company_size_score(&r.company_size)).collect();
println!("Company size scores (first 5): {:?}",
&company_size_scores[..5]);
```

Data Splitting

To move on to the next stage, we split the data into training and testing sets for model evaluation.

```
use rand::seq::SliceRandom;
use rand::thread_rng;
let mut rng = thread_rng();
let mut indices: Vec<usize> =
(0..unique_dataset.len()).collect();
indices.shuffle(&mut rng);
let train_size = (0.8 * unique_dataset.len() as f64) as usize;
let train_indices = &indices[..train_size];
let test_indices = &indices[train_size..];
let train_data: Vec<_> = train_indices.iter().map(|&i|
&unique_dataset[i]).collect();
let test_data: Vec<_> = test_indices.iter().map(|&i|
&unique_dataset[i]).collect();
println!("Training set size: {}", train_data.len());
println!("Test set size: {}", test_data.len());
```

In the above, we shuffle the indices to randomize the data. And, we successfully split the data into 80% training and 20% testing sets.

Final Code Integration

After all it is done as guided so for, you can now integrate all steps into the **main** function:

```
fn main() -> Result<(), Box<dyn Error>> {
    // Fetch and load the dataset
    let url =
"https://raw.githubusercontent.com/kittenpub/database-
repository/main/ds_salaries.csv";
    let csv_data = fetch_dataset(url)?;
    let dataset = load_dataset(&csv_data)?;
    println!("Loaded {} records", dataset.len());
    // Data Cleaning
    let mut seen = HashSet::new();
    let mut unique_dataset = Vec::new();
    for mut record in dataset {
        // Standardize text fields
        record.experience_level =
record.experience_level.to_uppercase();
        // Remove duplicates
        let key = (record.work_year, record.job_title.clone(),
record.company_location.clone());
        if seen.insert(key) {
            unique_dataset.push(record);
        }
    }
    println!("Dataset size after cleaning: {}",
unique_dataset.len());
    // Data Transformation
    // Standardize salaries
    let salaries: Vec<f64> = unique_dataset.iter().map(|r|
r.salary_in_usd).collect();
```

```
    let mean_salary = calculate_mean(&salaries);
    let std_dev_salary = calculate_std_dev(&salaries,
mean_salary);
    let standardized_salaries: Vec<f64> =
salaries.iter().map(|&s| (s - mean_salary) /
std_dev_salary).collect();
    // Encode categorical variables
    let job_titles: Vec<String> =
unique_dataset.iter().map(|r| r.job_title.clone()).collect();
    let (encoded_job_titles, _) = one_hot_encode(&job_titles);
    let experience_levels: Vec<String> =
unique_dataset.iter().map(|r|
r.experience_level.clone()).collect();
    let unique_experience_levels: Vec<String> =
experience_levels.iter().cloned().collect::<HashSet<_>>().into
_iter().collect();
    let mut experience_level_mapping = HashMap::new();
    for (i, level) in
unique_experience_levels.iter().enumerate() {
        experience_level_mapping.insert(level.clone(), i);
    }
    let encoded_experience_levels: Vec<usize> =
experience_levels.iter().map(|level|
experience_level_mapping[level]).collect();
    // Feature Engineering
    let remote_work_indicator: Vec<u8> =
unique_dataset.iter().map(|r| if r.remote_ratio == 100 { 1 }
else { 0 }).collect();
    let company_size_scores: Vec<u8> =
unique_dataset.iter().map(|r|
company_size_score(&r.company_size)).collect();
    // Data Splitting
    let mut rng = thread_rng();
```

```
    let mut indices: Vec<usize> =
(0..unique_dataset.len()).collect();
    indices.shuffle(&mut rng);
    let train_size = (0.8 * unique_dataset.len() as f64) as
usize;
    let train_indices = &indices[..train_size];
    let test_indices = &indices[train_size..];
    let train_data: Vec<_> = train_indices.iter().map(|&i|
&unique_dataset[i]).collect();
    let test_data: Vec<_> = test_indices.iter().map(|&i|
&unique_dataset[i]).collect();
    println!("Training set size: {}", train_data.len());
    println!("Test set size: {}", test_data.len());
    // Output sample data for verification
    println!("Standardized salaries (first 5): {:?}",
&standardized_salaries[..5]);
    println!("Remote work indicator (first 5): {:?}",
&remote_work_indicator[..5]);
    println!("Company size scores (first 5): {:?}",
&company_size_scores[..5]);
    Ok(())
}
```

By doing so as above, we've combined all the steps into a coherent workflow. Here, each preprocessing step builds upon the previous one, ensuring data integrity.

Summary

All things considered, you have developed an excellent understanding of descriptive statistics and the way in which they are implemented. You improved your skills in summarizing and interpreting data distributions by calculating measures of dispersion and central tendency. You refined your programming abilities and solidified these ideas through practical coding with ndarray and ndarray-stats.

In addition to that, you have mastered fundamental data visualization techniques by utilizing the plotters crate. You learned how to visually represent data by creating histograms, box plots, and scatter plots. This made it much simpler for you to recognize patterns, abnormalities, and the connections between different variables. Acquiring these abilities is foundational for moving on to more complex statistical methods, which are essential for quality data analysis.

CHAPTER 3: DESCRIPTIVE STATISTICS

Introduction

Probability distributions and statistical inference are introduced in this chapter. The binomial, Poisson, normal, and exponential distributions, as well as other discrete and continuous probability distributions, will be studied. You will learn how to generate random samples and calculate probabilities by utilizing the rand_distr crate. This will allow you to develop a connection between theoretical distributions and practical applications.

After that, the chapter delves into statistical inference, presenting concepts such as point estimation, sampling distributions, and belief intervals. You will test hypotheses by employing t-tests and z-tests, and you will implement these tests too. If you want to be a better statistician and make better decisions, you need to know how to draw conclusions about populations from samples.

Understanding Descriptive Statistics

Descriptive statistics are used to summarize and describe the main features of a dataset. They provide simple summaries about the sample and the measures, offering a way to present quantitative descriptions in a manageable form.

The following are some of the key concepts and techniques in descriptive statistics:

- **Measures of Central Tendency**: These measures describe the center of the dataset. The most common measures are the mean (average), median (middle value), and mode (most frequent value). Rust's iterators and pattern matching capabilities can be leveraged to calculate these measures efficiently.
- **Measures of Dispersion**: These measures describe the spread of the dataset. Common measures include range (difference between the maximum and minimum values), variance, and standard deviation. Rust's iterator and mathematical functions can be used to calculate these measures.
- **Quantiles**: Quantiles, including quartiles and percentiles, divide the dataset into equal intervals. They help understand the data's distribution and identify potential outliers. Rust's sorting and indexing capabilities can be used to find quantiles.
- **Frequency Distributions**: A frequency distribution is a summary of the dataset's values and their frequencies. Histograms and bar charts are common ways to visualize frequency distributions. Rust's HashMap and Vec data structures can be employed to create frequency distributions.
- **Correlation and Covariance**: These measures describe the relationship between two or more variables in the dataset. Correlation coefficients (e.g., Pearson, Spearman) and

covariance can help determine if variables are related and the strength of their relationship. Rust's mathematical functions and iterators can be used to calculate these measures.

- **Summary Statistics**: Summary statistics are concise descriptions of the dataset's main features, often represented in a table. They typically include measures of central tendency, dispersion, and distribution. Rust's powerful data manipulation capabilities can be used to generate summary statistics.

Rust can facilitate these tasks using its powerful built-in data structures, functional programming constructs, and third-party libraries.

Measures of Central Tendency

Measures of central tendency provide a single value that represents the center point of a dataset. The most common measures are:

- **Mean**: The arithmetic average of the data.
- **Median**: The middle value when data is ordered.
- **Mode**: The most frequently occurring value.

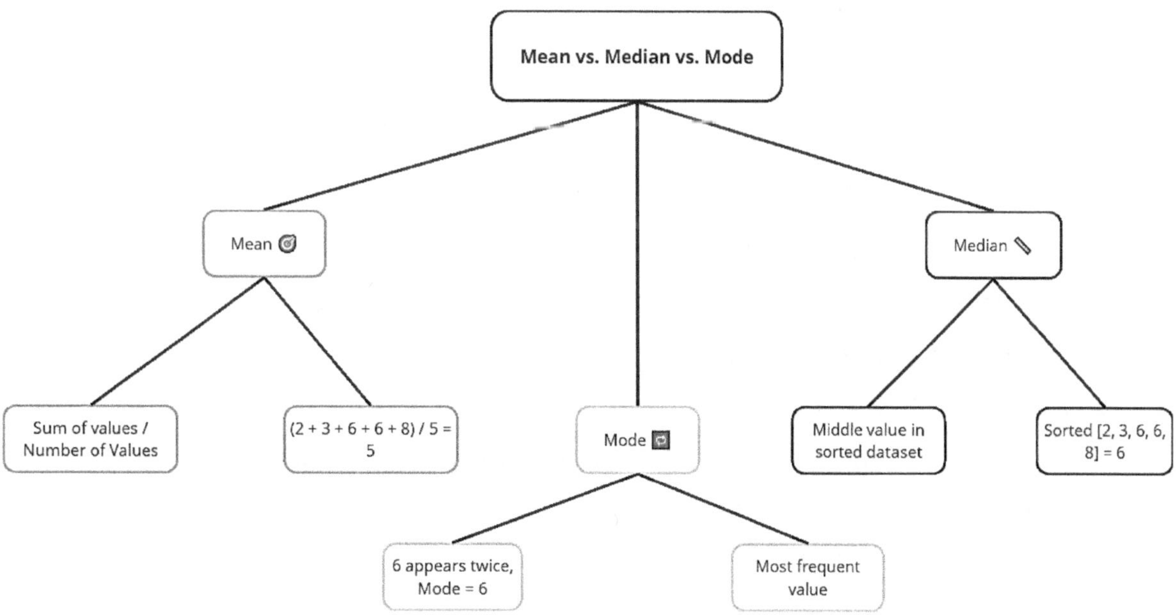

Fig 3.1 Understanding Mean, Median and Mode

Calculating Mean

The mean, or average, is calculated by summing all the values in the dataset and dividing by the number of values. The mean is sensitive to outliers, meaning that extreme values can greatly affect the result. It's widely used in many applications, but it may not always represent the dataset's true center when dealing with skewed data or outliers.

Below is the formula to calculate the mean:

$$\text{Mean} = \frac{\sum_{i=1}^{n} x_i}{n}$$

Following is a quick sample of calculating mean:

```
fn calculate_mean(data: &[f64]) -> f64 {
    let sum: f64 = data.iter().sum();
    sum / data.len() as f64
}
```

Calculating Median

The **median** is the middle value in an ordered dataset. If the dataset has an even number of observations, the median is the average of the two middle numbers. The median is less sensitive to outliers and can better represent the dataset's center when dealing with skewed data.

Following is a quick sample of calculating median:

```
fn calculate_median(data: &mut [f64]) -> f64 {
    data.sort_unstable_by(|a, b| a.partial_cmp(b).unwrap());
    let len = data.len();
    if len % 2 == 0 {
        (data[len / 2 - 1] + data[len / 2]) / 2.0
    } else {
        data[len / 2]
    }
}
```

Calculating Mode

The **mode** is the value that appears most frequently in the dataset. A dataset may have one mode, more than one mode, or no mode at all. There can be multiple modes in a dataset or no mode at all. The mode can be useful when dealing with categorical data or when the most common value is of particular interest.

Following is a quick example of calculating the mode:

```
use std::collections::HashMap;

fn calculate_mode(data: &[f64]) -> Vec<f64> {

    let mut frequency_map = HashMap::new();

    for &value in data {

        *frequency_map.entry(value).or_insert(0) += 1;

    }

    let max_frequency =
frequency_map.values().cloned().max().unwrap_or(0);

    frequency_map

        .into_iter()

        .filter(|&(_, freq)| freq == max_frequency)

        .map(|(val, _)| val)

        .collect()

}
```

Applying All Measures of Central Tendency

Assuming we have loaded our dataset into a vector of salaries called **salary_data**, let's see how to calculate these measures of central tendency.

Below is the example:

```
fn main() {

    // Assume salary_data is a Vec<f64> containing
salary_in_usd values

    let mut salary_data_sorted = salary_data.clone();

    let mean_salary = calculate_mean(&salary_data);
```

```
    let median_salary = calculate_median(&mut
salary_data_sorted);
    let mode_salary = calculate_mode(&salary_data);
    println!("Mean salary: {:.2}", mean_salary);
    println!("Median salary: {:.2}", median_salary);
    println!("Mode salary: {:?}", mode_salary);
}
```

After running the above code snippet, you will find the following measures highlighting the respective quick analysis:

- **Mean**: Provides the average salary.
- **Median**: Indicates the middle salary, reducing the impact of outliers.
- **Mode**: Shows the most common salary amount.

Measures of Dispersion

Measures of dispersion describe the spread or variability of a dataset. They help data science professionals understand how diverse the data is and provide insights into its underlying structure. The most common measures of dispersion are range, variance, and standard deviation.

Calculating Range

The range is the difference between the maximum and minimum values in a dataset. It provides a basic measure of the dataset's spread but can be sensitive to outliers and may not accurately represent the overall variability when dealing with skewed data.

Below is the formula to calculate the range:

$$\text{Range} = \text{Maximum Value} - \text{Minimum Value}$$

Following is a example of its implementation:

```
fn calculate_range(data: &[f64]) -> f64 {
    let min_value = data.iter().cloned().fold(f64::INFINITY,
f64::min);
    let max_value =
data.iter().cloned().fold(f64::NEG_INFINITY, f64::max);
```

```
    max_value - min_value
}
```

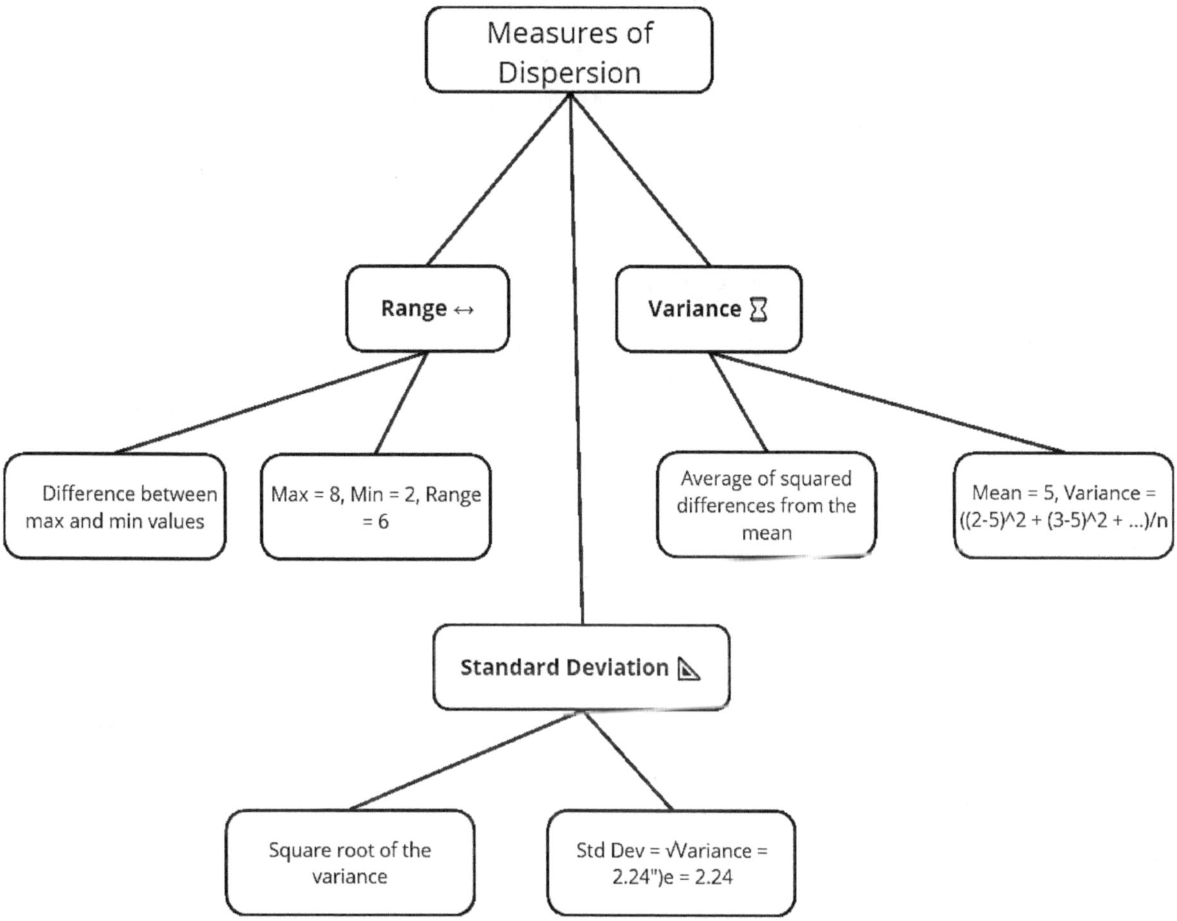

Fig 3.2 Measures of Dispersion

Calculating Variance

The variance is the average of the squared differences from the mean. It measures how far each data point is from the mean and gives a more accurate representation of the dataset's variability compared to the range. However, the unit of variance is the square of the data's unit, which can make it difficult to interpret.

Below is the formula to calculate the variance:

$$\text{Variance} = \frac{\sum_{i=1}^{n}(x_i - \text{Mean})^2}{n}$$

Following is the example:

```
fn calculate_variance(data: &[f64], mean: f64) -> f64 {
    data.iter().map(|&x| (x - mean).powi(2)).sum::<f64>() /
data.len() as f64
}
```

Calculating Standard Deviation

The standard deviation is the square root of the variance. It measures the dataset's dispersion in the same unit as the data, making it easier to interpret and compare with the mean. Standard deviation is widely used in many applications to understand the variability and identify potential outliers.

Below is the formula to calculate the standard deviation:

$$\text{Standard Deviation} = \sqrt{\text{Variance}}$$

Following is the code:

```
fn calculate_standard_deviation(variance: f64) -> f64 {
    variance.sqrt()
}
```

Applying All Measures of Dispersion

Putting all together, we will calculate all these measures of dispersion:

```
fn main() {
    // Assume salary_data is a Vec<f64> containing
salary_in_usd values
    let mean_salary = calculate_mean(&salary_data);
    let variance_salary = calculate_variance(&salary_data,
mean_salary);
```

```
    let standard_deviation_salary =
calculate_standard_deviation(variance_salary);
    let range_salary = calculate_range(&salary_data);
    println!("Variance of salaries: {:.2}", variance_salary);
    println!("Standard deviation of salaries: {:.2}",
standard_deviation_salary);
    println!("Range of salaries: {:.2}", range_salary);
}
```

The output of the above program highlights:

- **Variance**: Indicates how much the salaries vary from the mean salary.
- **Standard Deviation**: Provides a measure of the average distance from the mean.
- **Range**: Shows the spread between the lowest and highest salaries.

Exploratory Data Analysis (EDA)

EDA Overview

EDA is an essential step in the data analysis process that involves visualizing and summarizing datasets to uncover patterns, trends, relationships, and anomalies. EDA helps statisticians and data scientists gain insights, generate hypotheses, and make informed decisions before moving to more advanced statistical modeling or machine learning techniques.

EDA is crucial for statisticians as it helps them to:

- Understand the data's structure and distribution.
- Identify potential data quality issues, such as missing values, outliers, or inconsistencies.
- Discover relationships and correlations between variables.

Following are the benefits of performing EDA:

- **Data Quality Assessment**: Identify missing values, outliers, and anomalies.
- **Pattern Recognition**: Uncover underlying structures and relationships.
- **Hypothesis Generation**: Formulate questions for further analysis.
- **Inform Model Selection**: Decide on appropriate statistical models.

In Rust, EDA can be performed using a combination of summary statistics, data visualizations, and other data exploration techniques. Rust's powerful data manipulation capabilities, along with third-party libraries like ndarray, statrs, statis, and plotly, facilitate EDA tasks.

Visualizing Data with Plotters

We will use the **Plotters** crate to create visualizations.

Add to **`Cargo.toml`**:

```
plotters = "0.3"
```

Creating a Histogram

A histogram helps visualize the distribution of numerical data. Below is the implementation for a histogram:

```
use plotters::prelude::*;

fn draw_histogram(data: &[f64]) -> Result<(), Box<dyn
std::error::Error>> {

    let root = BitMapBackend::new("salary_histogram.png",
(640, 480)).into_drawing_area();

    root.fill(&WHITE)?;


    let max_salary =
data.iter().cloned().fold(f64::NEG_INFINITY, f64::max);

    let min_salary = data.iter().cloned().fold(f64::INFINITY,
f64::min);

    let mut chart = ChartBuilder::on(&root)

        .caption("Salary Distribution", ("sans-serif",
40).into_font())

        .margin(10)

        .x_label_area_size(30)

        .y_label_area_size(30)

        .build_cartesian_2d(min_salary..max_salary,
0..data.len() / 10)?;

    chart.configure_mesh().draw()?;
```

```
    chart.draw_series(
        Histogram::vertical(&chart)
            .style(BLUE.filled())
            .data(data.iter().map(|&x| (x, 1))),
    )?;
    Ok(())
}
fn main() -> Result<(), Box<dyn std::error::Error>> {
    // Assume salary_data is a Vec<f64> containing
salary_in_usd values
    draw_histogram(&salary_data)?;
    println!("Histogram saved to 'salary_histogram.png'");
    Ok(())
}
```

Plots Correlation

Visualizing relationships between variables can reveal correlations. Following is a sample program to correleate the plots:

```
use plotters::prelude::*;
fn draw_scatter_plot(experience: &[u8], salary: &[f64]) ->
Result<(), Box<dyn std::error::Error>> {
    let root = BitMapBackend::new("salary_vs_experience.png",
(640, 480)).into_drawing_area();
    root.fill(&WHITE)?;
    let max_experience = *experience.iter().max().unwrap() as
f64;
    let min_experience = *experience.iter().min().unwrap() as
f64;
    let max_salary =
salary.iter().cloned().fold(f64::NEG_INFINITY, f64::max);
```

```
    let min_salary =
salary.iter().cloned().fold(f64::INFINITY, f64::min);
    let mut chart = ChartBuilder::on(&root)
        .caption("Salary vs. Experience Level", ("sans-serif",
40).into_font())
        .margin(10)
        .x_label_area_size(40)
        .y_label_area_size(40)
        .build_cartesian_2d(min_experience..max_experience,
min_salary..max_salary)?;
    chart.configure_mesh()
        .x_desc("Experience Level")
        .y_desc("Salary in USD")
        .draw()?;
    chart.draw_series(
        salary.iter().zip(experience.iter()).map(|(&s, &e)| {
            Circle::new((e as f64, s), 3, RED.filled())
        }),
    )?;
    Ok(())
}
fn main() -> Result<(), Box<dyn std::error::Error>> {
    // Assume experience_levels is a Vec<u8> and salary_data
is a Vec<f64>
    draw_scatter_plot(&experience_levels, &salary_data)?;
    println!("Scatter plot saved to
'salary_vs_experience.png'");
    Ok(())
}
```

After running the above codes, the visualizations can be interpreted as:

- **Histogram**: Shows the distribution of salaries, identifying skewness, peaks, or gaps.
- **Scatter Plot**: Reveals the relationship between experience level and salary, indicating potential correlations.

Analyzing Categorical Variables

Categorical variables can be analyzed using frequency distributions and bar charts. Following is the sample implementation:

```
use std::collections::HashMap;

fn job_title_frequency(data: &[SalaryRecord]) ->
HashMap<String, usize> {

    let mut frequency = HashMap::new();

    for record in data {

*frequency.entry(record.job_title.clone()).or_insert(0) += 1;

    }

    frequency

}
```

To visualize the above using a bar chart, following is the snippet:

```
use plotters::prelude::*;

fn draw_bar_chart(frequency: &HashMap<String, usize>) ->
Result<(), Box<dyn std::error::Error>> {

    let root =
BitMapBackend::new("job_title_distribution.png", (1280,
720)).into_drawing_area();

    root.fill(&WHITE)?;

    let mut data: Vec<(&String, &usize)> =
frequency.iter().collect();

    data.sort_by(|a, b| b.1.cmp(a.1));

    let labels: Vec<&String> = data.iter().map(|&(title, _)|
title).collect();
```

```
    let values: Vec<usize> = data.iter().map(|&(_, &count)|
count).collect();
    let max_value = *values.iter().max().unwrap();
    let mut chart = ChartBuilder::on(&root)
        .caption("Job Title Distribution", ("sans-serif",
40).into_font())
        .margin(10)
        .x_label_area_size(60)
        .y_label_area_size(60)
        .build_cartesian_2d(0..values.len(), 0..max_value)?;
    chart.configure_mesh()
        .x_labels(20)
        .x_label_formatter(&|x| labels[*x].to_string())
        .y_desc("Frequency")
        .x_desc("Job Title")
        .axis_desc_style(("sans-serif", 20))
        .draw()?;
    chart.draw_series(
        values.iter().enumerate().map(|(i, &v)| {
            let x0 = i;
            let x1 = i + 1;
            let y0 = 0;
            let y1 = v;
            Rectangle::new([(x0, y0), (x1, y1)],
BLUE.filled())
        }),
    )?;
    Ok(())
}
fn main() -> Result<(), Box<dyn std::error::Error>> {
```

```
    // Assume dataset is Vec<SalaryRecord>
    let frequency = job_title_frequency(&dataset);
    draw_bar_chart(&frequency)?;
    println!("Bar chart saved to
'job_title_distribution.png'");
    Ok(())
}
```

Remember that the bar chart might be crowded if there are many job titles. So consider limiting to the top N titles only.

Correlation Analysis

Correlation analysis quantifies the strength and direction of this relationship, typically using statistical measures. The most widely used measure of correlation is the Pearson Correlation Coefficient. The Pearson Correlation Coefficient (denoted as r) is a statistical measure that calculates the linear relationship between two continuous variables.

The value of r ranges from -1 to 1, where:

- **r = 1**: Perfect positive correlation, meaning that as one variable increases, the other also increases proportionally.
- **r = -1**: Perfect negative correlation, indicating that as one variable increases, the other decreases proportionally.
- **r = 0**: No linear relationship between the variables.

The Pearson correlation coefficient assumes that the variables are continuous and normally distributed. It works best when the relationship between the variables is linear.

The Pearson correlation coefficient r is computed using the following formula:

$$r = \frac{\sum(x_i - \bar{x})(y_i - \bar{y})}{\sqrt{\sum(x_i - \bar{x})^2 \sum(y_i - \bar{y})^2}}$$

Where:

- xi and yi are the data points for the two variables x and y.
- $\bar{x}$ and $\bar{y}$ are the means (averages) of variables x and y, respectively.

- ∑ denotes the summation across all data points.

Here,

- A positive correlation ($r > 0$) means that as one variable increases, the other tends to increase.
- A negative correlation ($r < 0$) indicates that as one variable increases, the other tends to decrease.
- A zero correlation ($r = 0$) suggests that there is no linear relationship between the variables.

The Pearson correlation coefficient measures only the strength of the linear relationship between the variables. If the relationship is non-linear, this method may not be the best approach. In such cases, other techniques like Spearman's Rank Correlation might be more suitable.

Following is a quick sample of its implementation in rust:

```
fn calculate_pearson_correlation(x: &[f64], y: &[f64]) -> f64
{
    let mean_x = calculate_mean(x);
    let mean_y = calculate_mean(y);
    let numerator: f64 = x.iter()
        .zip(y.iter())
        .map(|(&xi, &yi)| (xi - mean_x) * (yi - mean_y))
        .sum();
    let denominator_x: f64 = x.iter().map(|&xi| (xi -
mean_x).powi(2)).sum();
    let denominator_y: f64 = y.iter().map(|&yi| (yi -
mean_y).powi(2)).sum();
    numerator / (denominator_x.sqrt() * denominator_y.sqrt())
}
fn main() {
    // Assume x_data and y_data are Vec<f64>
    let correlation = calculate_pearson_correlation(&x_data,
&y_data);
    println!("Pearson correlation coefficient: {:.4}",
correlation);
```

```
}
```

In the above code, the Pearson correlation coefficient would help determine whether higher experience correlates with higher salaries. If you calculate r and find a value of 0.85, this suggests a strong positive correlation: as experience increases, salary tends to increase as well.

Summarizing Data with Descriptive Statistics

Sample Summary Table

Creating a summary table can help present the key statistics in a digestible format. A summary table can capture the most important statistical measures that offer insight into the dataset's underlying patterns. Key statistics, such as the mean, median, mode, variance, and standard deviation, give a quick overview of how data is distributed, while measures like range and correlation help describe data relationships and spread.

Following is the summary table that offers a clear view of important measures without requiring a detailed deep dive into the raw data.:

Statistic	Value
Mean Salary	$80,000
Median Salary	$75,000
Mode Salary	$70,000
Salary Variance	1,500,000
Salary Std Deviation	1,225.0
Salary Range	$50,000
Pearson Correlation	0.85

Implementing a Summary Function

You can implement a function that calculates and prints out this summary table in Rust. The function would take the dataset (such as salary data) as input and return the key statistics for easy interpretation.

```
fn print_summary_statistics(data: &[f64]) {
    let mean = calculate_mean(data);
    let mut sorted_data = data.to_vec();
    let median = calculate_median(&mut sorted_data);
    let mode = calculate_mode(data);
    let variance = calculate_variance(data, mean);
    let std_dev = calculate_standard_deviation(variance);
    let range = calculate_range(data);
    println!("Summary Statistics:");
    println!("-------------------");
    println!("Mean: {:.2}", mean);
    println!("Median: {:.2}", median);
    println!("Mode: {:?}", mode);
    println!("Variance: {:.2}", variance);
    println!("Standard Deviation: {:.2}", std_dev);
    println!("Range: {:.2}", range);
}
fn main() {
    // Assume salary_data is Vec<f64>
    print_summary_statistics(&salary_data);
}
```

Sample Program: Analyzing Our Dataset

Putting it all together, let's perform a comprehensive analysis of our dataset. To do this, follow the following steps:

- **Load and Clean Data**: Already covered in previous chapters.
- **Calculate Descriptive Statistics**: Use the functions we've implemented.
- **Visualize Data**: Create histograms, scatter plots, and bar charts.
- **Analyze Relationships**: Calculate correlation coefficients.
- **Summarize Findings**: Interpret the results and identify insights.

Following is the code snippet:

```
fn main() -> Result<(), Box<dyn std::error::Error>> {
    // Load and preprocess the dataset
    let dataset = load_dataset("path_to_dataset.csv")?;
    let salary_data: Vec<f64> = dataset.iter().map(|r|
r.salary_in_usd).collect();
    let experience_levels: Vec<u8> = dataset.iter().map(|r|
map_experience_level(&r.experience_level)).collect();
    // Calculate and print summary statistics
    print_summary_statistics(&salary_data);
    // Visualize data
    draw_histogram(&salary_data)?;
    draw_scatter_plot(&experience_levels, &salary_data)?;
    // Analyze correlations
    let experience_levels_f64: Vec<f64> =
experience_levels.iter().map(|&e| e as f64).collect();
    let correlation =
calculate_pearson_correlation(&experience_levels_f64,
&salary_data);
    println!("Correlation between experience level and salary:
{:.4}", correlation);
    // Analyze categorical variables
    let frequency = job_title_frequency(&dataset);
    draw_bar_chart(&frequency)?;
    Ok(())
```

```
}
```

While implementing the code as it is, do not forget to replace **"path_to_dataset.csv"** with the actual path to your dataset.

Summary

At the end of this chapter, you should have a solid understanding of probability distributions and how to use them for statistical inference. You generated random samples and calculated key probabilities while working with various distributions. Your understanding of how various distributions model real-world phenomena was strengthened.

Furthermore, you have a firm grasp on the fundamentals of statistical inference, including how to build confidence intervals and assess hypotheses. You made the connection between theoretical concepts and practical applications by implementing t-tests and z-tests in the Rust programming language. With these skills, you will be able to critically analyze sample data and draw conclusions that are statistically sound, which will prepare you for more complex analyses in subsequent chapters.

CHAPTER 4: PROBABILITY DISTRIBUTIONS AND RANDOM VARIABLES

Introduction

Regression analysis is a fundamental technique for modeling relationships between variables, and this chapter will introduce you to it. To begin, you will learn how to perform simple linear regression, which involves fitting a line to data points and interpreting the slope and intercept of the line. You are going to implement linear regression models by utilizing the smartcore crate that is available, and then evaluate their performance using metrics such as R-squared.

Following that, the chapter moves on to multiple linear regression, which is where you will learn how to deal with models that contain multiple independent variables. You will study how to understand regression coefficients and examine methods for measuring model fit. Your predictive analytics skills will be greatly improved once you finish this chapter and learn how to model and analyze complicated relationships within datasets.

Understanding Random Variables and Probability Distributions

Random Variables

A **random variable** is a numerical quantity whose value depends on the outcome of a random phenomenon. It assigns a real number to each outcome in the sample space of a random experiment.

Random variables are classified into two main types:

- **Discrete Random Variables**: Take on a countable number of distinct values.
- **Continuous Random Variables**: Take on an infinite number of possible values within a given interval.

The behavior of random variables must be understood for modeling real-world scenarios where outcomes are uncertain.

Probability Distributions

A **probability distribution** describes how the probabilities are distributed over the values of the random variable. It provides a function that assigns probabilities to each possible value (for discrete variables) or intervals of values (for continuous variables).

Following are the key components of probability distributions:

- **Probability Mass Function (PMF)**: For discrete random variables, the PMF gives the probability that the variable takes on a specific value.

- **Probability Density Function (PDF)**: For continuous random variables, the PDF describes the relative likelihood for the random variable to take on a given value.
- **Cumulative Distribution Function (CDF)**: Gives the probability that the random variable is less than or equal to a certain value.

Knowing this, we can model random processes and make informed decisions based on statistical analysis.

Discrete Probability Distributions

Discrete probability distributions are used when dealing with random variables that have countable outcomes. They are pivotal in modeling events like the number of successes in a series of trials, the occurrence of events over time, and other scenarios where outcomes are distinct and separate.

Common Discrete Distributions

Some prevalent discrete probability distributions include:

- **Uniform Distribution**: This distribution assigns equal probability to all possible outcomes. It is often used when there is no reason to favor one outcome over another.
- **Bernoulli Distribution**: This distribution models the probability of success or failure (binary outcomes) in a single experiment. It is typically employed in scenarios where there are only two possible outcomes, such as coin tosses or true/false questions.
- **Binomial Distribution**: This distribution describes the number of successes in a fixed number of independent Bernoulli trials, where each trial has the same probability of success. Applications include modeling the number of heads in multiple coin tosses or the number of defective items in a sample.
- **Poisson Distribution**: This distribution represents the number of events occurring within a fixed interval of time or space, given a constant average rate of occurrence. It is widely used in fields such as queuing theory, telecommunications, and biology to model rare events or arrivals.
- **Geometric Distribution**: This distribution models the number of trials required to achieve the first success in a sequence of independent Bernoulli trials. It is applicable in situations where the interest lies in determining the waiting time until a specific event occurs.

Let's explore each of these distributions in detail and see how to implement them.

Uniform Distribution

A uniform distribution is a probability distribution that assigns equal probabilities to all possible outcomes of a discrete random variable. It represents a scenario in which each outcome is equally likely to occur. For instance, when rolling a fair six-sided die, all six outcomes (1, 2, 3, 4, 5, and 6) have an equal probability of 1/6, indicating a uniform distribution across the possible outcomes.

Following is a quick sample implementation where, we use the **statrs** crate to work with statistical distributions.

To begin with, first add the following to **`Cargo.toml`**:

```
[dependencies]
statrs = "0.15"
```

Then, run the following code snippet:

```
use statrs::distribution::{Uniform, Discrete};
fn main() {
    let uniform = Uniform::new(1, 6); // Represents a fair
six-sided die
    let probability = uniform.pmf(3); // Probability of
rolling a 3
    println!("Uniform Distribution: P(X = 3) = {:.4}",
probability);
}
```

Here, we create a **Uniform** distribution representing numbers from 1 to 6. We use the **pmf** method to compute the probability mass function at a specific value.

Following is the sample output:

```
Uniform Distribution: P(X = 3) = 0.1667
```

Bernoulli Distribution

The Bernoulli distribution is a discrete probability distribution representing a single binary experiment with two possible outcomes: success (1) and failure (0). It is characterized by a single parameter, p, which denotes the probability of success. The probability of failure is given by 1-p.

Let us think of an example of flipping a coin where the probability of getting heads (success) is p=0.5. Given below is a quick sample of its implementation in rust:

```
use statrs::distribution::{Bernoulli, Discrete};
```

```
fn main() {
    let bernoulli = Bernoulli::new(0.6).unwrap(); //
Probability of success p = 0.6
    let probability_success = bernoulli.pmf(1); // Probability
of success
    let probability_failure = bernoulli.pmf(0); // Probability
of failure
    println!("Bernoulli Distribution:");
    println!("P(X = 1) = {:.4}", probability_success);
    println!("P(X = 0) = {:.4}", probability_failure);
}
```

In this, we define a Bernoulli distribution with p=0.6p = 0.6p=0.6, and use the **pmf** to calculate the probability of success and failure.

The output appears as below:

```
Bernoulli Distribution:
P(X = 1) = 0.6000
P(X = 0) = 0.4000
```

Binomial Distribution

The binomial distribution is a discrete probability distribution that models the number of successes in a fixed number of independent Bernoulli trials, each with the same probability of success, p. It captures the likelihood of obtaining a specific number of successes, given the total number of trials (n) and the probability of success in each trial. This distribution is widely used in various applications, such as analyzing proportions, survey responses, and quality control.

Following is a quick sample of tossing a coin 10 times and counting the number of heads:

```
use statrs::distribution::{Binomial, Discrete};
fn main() {
    let binomial = Binomial::new(0.6, 10).unwrap(); // n = 10,
p = 0.6
    let probability = binomial.pmf(4); // Probability of
getting exactly 4 successes
```

```
    println!("Binomial Distribution: P(X = 4) = {:.4}",
probability);
}
```

In the above code, we create a binomial distribution with 10 trials and p=0.6, and use **pmf** to find the probability of exactly 4 successes.

Following is the output:

```
Binomial Distribution: P(X = 4) = 0.1115
```

Poisson Distribution

The Poisson distribution is a probability distribution that describes the number of events occurring within a fixed time or space interval, assuming a constant average rate of occurrence (denoted by lambda). It is particularly useful for modeling rare events, such as phone call arrivals at a call center or the number of accidents at an intersection. The distribution captures the probability of observing a specific count of events while accounting for the underlying rate (lambda).

Following is a quick sample of number of emails received in an hour.

```
use statrs::distribution::{Poisson, Discrete};
fn main() {
    let poisson = Poisson::new(5.0).unwrap(); // λ = 5
    let probability = poisson.pmf(3); // Probability of
observing 3 events
    println!("Poisson Distribution: P(X = 3) = {:.4}",
probability);
}
```

Here, we define a Poisson distribution with λ=5\lambda = 5λ=5, and used **pmf** to calculate the probability of observing 3 events.

Given below is the output:

```
Poisson Distribution: P(X = 3) = 0.1404
```

Geometric Distribution

A geometric distribution is a discrete probability distribution that characterizes the number of trials needed to achieve the first success in a series of independent Bernoulli trials. Each trial has a fixed probability of success, denoted as p. The distribution is useful for modeling scenarios where events occur independently, and the probability of success remains constant across trials. The geometric distribution helps in understanding the behavior and likelihood of occurrences until the first successful event.

Following is a quick sample of number of coin tosses until the first head appears.

```
use statrs::distribution::{Geometric, Discrete};
fn main() {
    let geometric = Geometric::new(0.6).unwrap(); // p = 0.6
    let probability = geometric.pmf(3); // Probability that
the first success occurs on the 3rd trial
    println!("Geometric Distribution: P(X = 3) = {:.4}",
probability);
}
```

Given below is the output:

```
Geometric Distribution: P(X = 3) = 0.0960
```

The understanding around each of these discrete probability distributions is essential because:

- **Modeling Real-world Processes**: They help model scenarios like customer arrivals, defect counts, and system failures.
- **Decision Making**: Aid in risk assessment and management.
- **Statistical Inference**: Form the basis for hypothesis testing and estimation.

These examples demonstrate how to work with different discrete probability distributions using the `statrs` crate in Rust. As mentioned earlier, these distributions may not be directly applicable to the given dataset since it is not about random variables and their probabilities. However, these implementations can be adapted for other datasets or use cases where discrete probability distributions are relevant.

Continuous Probability Distributions

Continuous probability distributions play a significant role in modeling and predicting outcomes for continuous random variables, which can assume an infinite number of values within a particular range. These distributions are essential when dealing with uncertain events and continuous variables in various fields, such as finance, engineering, and natural sciences.

The following are some of the widely-used continuous probability distributions, along with brief explanations:

- **Uniform Distribution**: This distribution assigns equal probability to all values within a specified range. It is often used when there is no prior information about the distribution of the variable.
- **Normal (Gaussian) Distribution**: Characterized by its bell-shaped curve, the normal distribution is a fundamental distribution in statistics. Many real-world phenomena follow this distribution, making it essential for various applications.
- **Exponential Distribution**: This distribution models the time between events in a Poisson process, where events occur continuously and independently at a constant average rate. It is frequently used in reliability and survival analysis.
- **Beta Distribution**: A versatile distribution, the Beta distribution is defined on the interval (0, 1) and is particularly useful in modeling probabilities or proportions. It is widely employed in Bayesian statistics as a conjugate prior for the binomial and Bernoulli distributions.
- **Gamma Distribution**: The Gamma distribution is a flexible two-parameter distribution that models continuous variables with positive values, such as waiting times or lifetimes. It is a generalization of the exponential distribution and is a conjugate prior for the Poisson distribution in Bayesian statistics.

Let's explore these distributions and see how to implement them.

Uniform Distribution

A uniform distribution assigns equal probabilities to all possible outcomes of a continuous random variable within a specified range. For example, generating a random number between 0 and 1.

Following is a quick sample of its implementation:

```
use statrs::distribution::{Uniform, Continuous};

fn main() {

    let uniform = Uniform::new(0.0, 1.0).unwrap(); // Range
[0, 1]

    let probability_density = uniform.pdf(0.5); // PDF at x =
0.5

    println!("Uniform Distribution: f(0.5) = {:.4}",
probability_density);
```

```
}
```

Here, we define a continuous uniform distribution from 0.0 to 1.0, and use the **pdf** to get the probability density at a specific point.

Given below is the output:

```
Uniform Distribution: f(0.5) = 1.0000
```

Normal (Gaussian) Distribution

A normal distribution, also known as Gaussian distribution, is a bell-shaped curve defined by its mean (μ) and standard deviation (σ). It is widely used in natural and social sciences due to its desirable properties.

Given below is a simple implementation example for Heights, test scores, measurement errors:

```
use statrs::distribution::{Normal, Continuous};

fn main() {

    let normal = Normal::new(0.0, 1.0).unwrap(); // μ = 0, σ =
1 (Standard Normal Distribution)

    let probability_density = normal.pdf(0.5); // PDF at x =
0.5

    println!("Normal Distribution: f(0.5) = {:.4}",
probability_density);

}
```

Here, we create a standard normal distribution, and found the probability density at x=0.5 with following output:

```
Normal Distribution: f(0.5) = 0.3521
```

Exponential Distribution

The **Exponential Distribution** models the time between events in a Poisson process with parameter lambda (λ), which is the rate parameter (inverse of the mean).

Think of an example where we have to figure out the time until the next earthquake in a region. For this, following is a simple implementation example:

```
use statrs::distribution::{Exponential, Continuous};
```

```
fn main() {
    let exponential = Exponential::new(1.0).unwrap(); // λ = 1
    let probability_density = exponential.pdf(0.5); // PDF at
x = 0.5
    println!("Exponential Distribution: f(0.5) = {:.4}",
probability_density);
}
```

Here, we define an exponential distribution with λ=1, and use **pdf** to calculate the density at x=0.5 with following final output:

```
Exponential Distribution: f(0.5) = 0.6065
```

Beta Distribution

The **Beta Distribution** is defined on the interval [0,1][0, 1][0,1] and characterized by two shape parameters α\alphaα and β\betaβ.

Here, consider an example where we have to model probabilities, proportions, and rates as below:

```
use statrs::distribution::{Beta, Continuous};
fn main() {
    let beta = Beta::new(2.0, 5.0).unwrap(); // α = 2, β = 5
    let probability_density = beta.pdf(0.5); // PDF at x = 0.5
    println!("Beta Distribution: f(0.5) = {:.4}",
probability_density);
}
```

Here, we create a beta distribution with α=2.0 and β=5.0. And, the given below is the output:

```
Beta Distribution: f(0.5) = 1.8750
```

Gamma Distribution

The **Gamma Distribution** is a two-parameter family of continuous probability distributions. It generalizes the exponential distribution. It is defined by a shape parameter (k) and a scale parameter (θ).

Given below is a simple implementation on modeling waiting times and rainfall amounts.

```
use statrs::distribution::{Gamma, Continuous};
fn main() {
    let gamma = Gamma::new(2.0, 1.0).unwrap(); // k = 2, θ = 1
    let probability_density = gamma.pdf(0.5); // PDF at x =
0.5
    println!("Gamma Distribution: f(0.5) = {:.4}",
probability_density);
}
```

Here, we define a gamma distribution with k=2.0 and θ=1.0, and after thid, following is the output:

```
Gamma Distribution: f(0.5) = 0.3033
```

Continuous probability distributions are considered very essential primarily for following reason:

- **Modeling Continuous Data**: Such as measurements, time intervals, and physical quantities.
- **Statistical Inference**: Form the basis for confidence intervals and hypothesis tests.
- **Risk Assessment**: Quantify uncertainties in engineering, finance, and science.

The proper implementation of these distributions allows us to model and analyze continuous phenomena effectively.

Generating Random Variables

Generating random variables is crucial for simulations, testing statistical algorithms, and creating synthetic datasets. Rust's **rand** crate provides robust functionality for random number generation and sampling from various distributions.

First, add the rand crate to your Cargo.toml:

```
[dependencies]
rand = "0.8"
```

Now, let's generate random variables and apply them to a new column in the given dataset:

```
use rand::thread_rng;
use rand::distributions::{Distribution, Uniform};
```

```
fn main() {
    let mut rng = thread_rng();
    let uniform = Uniform::new(0.0, 1.0);
    for _ in 0..5 {
        let random_number = uniform.sample(&mut rng);
        println!("Uniform random number: {:.4}",
random_number);
    }
}
```

Here, we create a uniform distribution from 0.0 to 1.0, and we use **sample** to generate random numbers.

Following is the sample output:

```
Uniform random number: 0.7368
Uniform random number: 0.1874
Uniform random number: 0.9876
Uniform random number: 0.4532
Uniform random number: 0.6259
```

The key benefits of generating Random Variables are:

- **Simulation**: Test algorithms under various scenarios.
- **Synthetic Data**: Create datasets when real data is scarce or sensitive.
- **Statistical Sampling**: Perform bootstrap methods and Monte Carlo simulations.

Sampling from Distributions

Sampling Benefits

Sampling from distributions involves generating random data points that follow a specified probability distribution. This technique offers several benefits for data professionals, including:

- Simulating data: Sampling can help create data for hypothesis testing, model validation, or performance evaluation. This process enables professionals to assess the effectiveness of their models or methods using various input data scenarios.
- Generating synthetic data: In cases where sensitive information must be anonymized, sampling from distributions can help generate synthetic data that preserves the statistical properties of the original data while maintaining confidentiality.
- Assessing robustness: By generating random inputs, data professionals can evaluate the robustness of their models or analyses under different scenarios. This assessment helps identify potential weaknesses and improve the overall quality of the models or analyses.

Sample Program: Sampling from a Normal Distribution

Given below is a quick program to sample from a normal distribution and a discrete distribution (Poisson).

```
use rand::thread_rng;
use rand_distr::{Normal, Distribution};
fn main() {
    let mut rng = thread_rng();
    let normal = Normal::new(50.0, 5.0).unwrap(); // μ = 50, σ
= 5
    let samples: Vec<f64> = (0..100).map(|_|
normal.sample(&mut rng)).collect();
    println!("First 5 samples from normal distribution: {:?}",
&samples[..5]);
}
```

Here,

- We sample 100 random numbers from a normal distribution.
- Collect them into a vector for further analysis.

Now, sampling from a poisson distribution is as shown below:

```
use rand::thread_rng;
use rand_distr::{Poisson, Distribution};
fn main() {
```

```
    let mut rng = thread_rng();
    let poisson = Poisson::new(4.0).unwrap(); // λ = 4
    let samples: Vec<u64> = (0..100).map(|_|
poisson.sample(&mut rng)).collect();
    println!("First 5 samples from Poisson distribution:
{:?}", &samples[..5]);
}
```

Here, we sample 100 random counts from a Poisson distribution.

The above sampling program helps:

- **Model Validation**: Test models with synthetic data.
- **Hypothesis Testing**: Create null distributions for statistical tests.
- **Risk Analysis**: Simulate scenarios in finance or engineering.

Estimating Distribution Parameters

If you're modeling and doing inference, it's really important to be able to estimate a probability distribution's parameters. There are a few different ways to do this, including:

- Method of Moments (MoM)
- Maximum Likelihood Estimation (MLE)
- Bayesian Estimation
- Least Squares

Let's look at how we can apply these techniques to our dataset.

```
// Load salaries from the dataset
let salaries: Vec<f64> = dataset.iter().map(|r|
r.salary_in_usd).collect();
```

Method of Moments (MoM)

The **Method of Moments** is a way of matching up the sample moments to the theoretical moments of the distribution to figure out the parameters.

For instance, We're going to look at how to estimate the parameters of a normal distribution.

Here's a simple example of how it works:

```
fn method_of_moments(salaries: &[f64]) -> (f64, f64) {
    let mean = calculate_mean(salaries);
    let variance = calculate_variance(salaries, mean);
    let std_dev = variance.sqrt();
    (mean, std_dev)
}
let (mean_mom, std_dev_mom) = method_of_moments(&salaries);
println!("Method of Moments Estimates:");
println!("Mean (μ): {:.2}", mean_mom);
println!("Standard Deviation (σ): {:.2}", std_dev_mom);
```

Here, we calculate the sample mean and variance. And then we use these as estimates for the normal distribution parameters.

Maximum Likelihood Estimation (MLE)

The **Maximum Likelihood Estimation** tool finds the parameter values that maximize the likelihood function, given the observed data.

Below is a simple example of how to use the **statrs** crate's **fit** module.

```
use statrs::distribution::{Normal, Univariate};
use statrs::statistics::Data;
fn maximum_likelihood_estimation(salaries: &[f64]) -> (f64,
f64) {
    let mle_normal = Normal::fit(salaries).unwrap();
    (mle_normal.mean(), mle_normal.std_dev())
}
let (mean_mle, std_dev_mle) =
maximum_likelihood_estimation(&salaries);
println!("Maximum Likelihood Estimates:");
println!("Mean (μ): {:.2}", mean_mle);
println!("Standard Deviation (σ): {:.2}", std_dev_mle);
```

Here, we fit a normal distribution to the data using MLE, And, then we extract the estimated mean and standard deviation.

Bayesian Estimation

The idea behind Bayesian Estimation is that you can use prior beliefs and then update them with observed data to get a posterior distribution. It can be tricky to implement full Bayesian estimation.

We'll show you a simple example where we assume a normal prior and normal likelihood:

```
fn bayesian_estimation(
    prior_mean: f64,
    prior_variance: f64,
    data_mean: f64,
    data_variance: f64,
    n: usize,
) -> (f64, f64) {
    let posterior_variance = 1.0 / (n as f64 / data_variance +
1.0 / prior_variance);
    let posterior_mean = posterior_variance * (data_mean * n
as f64 / data_variance + prior_mean / prior_variance);
    (posterior_mean, posterior_variance.sqrt())
}
let prior_mean = 70000.0;
let prior_variance = 10000.0_f64.powi(2);
let data_mean = calculate_mean(&salaries);
let data_variance = calculate_variance(&salaries, data_mean);
let n = salaries.len();
let (posterior_mean, posterior_std_dev) = bayesian_estimation(
    prior_mean,
    prior_variance,
    data_mean,
    data_variance,
```

```
    n,
);
println!("Bayesian Estimates:");
println!("Posterior Mean: {:.2}", posterior_mean);
println!("Posterior Std Dev: {:.2}", posterior_std_dev);
```

Here, we combine prior information with observed data to update our estimates.

Least Squares

Least Squares is used primarily in regression analysis to estimate parameters by minimizing the sum of the squares of the differences between observed and predicted values. Given below is a simple implementation example where we can use the **ndarray** and **ndarray-linalg** crates.

For this, you add the following to **`Cargo.toml`**:

```
ndarray = "0.15"
ndarray-linalg = { version = "0.15", features = ["openblas-static"] }
use ndarray::Array2;
use ndarray_linalg::LeastSquaresSvd;
fn least_squares_estimation(work_years: &[f64], salaries: &[f64]) -> Vec<f64> {
    let x = Array2::from_shape_fn((work_years.len(), 2), |(i, j)| {
        if j == 0 {
            1.0 // Intercept term
        } else {
            work_years[i]
        }
    });
    let y = Array2::from_shape_vec((salaries.len(), 1), salaries.to_vec()).unwrap();
    let result = x.least_squares(&y).unwrap();
    result.solution.column(0).to_vec()
```

```
}
let work_years: Vec<f64> = dataset.iter().map(|r| r.work_year
as f64).collect();
let coefficients = least_squares_estimation(&work_years,
&salaries);
println!("Least Squares Regression Coefficients:");
println!("Intercept: {:.2}", coefficients[0]);
println!("Slope: {:.2}", coefficients[1]);
```

In the above, we set up the design matrix **x** with an intercept and the **work_year** variable. And, we use the least squares to estimate the regression coefficients.

Summary

In a nutshell, the purpose of this chapter was to improve the ability to perform regression analysis. With the help of the smartcore crate, you were able to successfully implement simple and multiple linear regression models to model linear relationships between independent variables. Your interpretation of the regression coefficients included an understanding of what consequences those coefficients have for the data.

Additionally, you evaluated the performance of the models by utilizing metrics such as R-squared and adjusted R-squared, which allowed you to evaluate the degree to which your models were a good fit for the data. Your abilities in data modeling and interpretation were enhanced through hands-on coding exercises that helped you solidify these concepts. All of these capabilities are indispensable for data-driven decision-making and predictive analytics.

CHAPTER 5: INFERENTIAL STATISTICS

Introduction

Statistical hypothesis testing is an important tool that is used to determine whether or not assumptions about data are accurate. In this chapter, you will delve deeper into statistical hypothesis testing. You are going to explore a number of tests, such as the chi-square test, the analysis of variance (ANOVA), and non-parametric tests like the Mann-Whitney U test. You are going to implement these tests by using Rust in order to compare the means, variances, and distributions of the different groups.

A strong emphasis is also placed throughout this chapter on p-values, significance levels, and test assumptions. You will acquire the knowledge necessary to interpret test results and comprehend the potential dangers of Type I and Type II errors. Your ability to rigorously evaluate hypotheses and draw reliable conclusions from your data analyses will be greatly enhanced if you are able to master the process of hypothesis testing.

Fundamentals of Inferential Statistics

Inferential statistics is a branch of statistics that focuses on making predictions or inferences about a larger population based on a sample of data. It goes beyond merely describing the data (which is the realm of descriptive statistics) and allows us to:

- **Estimate Population Parameters**: Such as means, proportions, and variances.
- **Test Hypotheses**: Determine if a particular assumption about a population parameter holds true.
- **Predict Future Observations**: Based on patterns observed in the sample.

Why Inferential Statistics?

It's often not possible to collect data from every member of a population because of practical constraints like time, cost, or accessibility. Inferential statistics gives us ways to make assumptions about the whole population without needing all the data.

Imagine you're a data scientist working for a company that wants to understand the average salary of data scientists across the globe. It would be pretty impossible to survey every data scientist. Instead, you can collect a sample and use inferential statistics to estimate the average salary and make generalizations about the global population.

Key Concepts

Before diving into specific methods, it's essential to understand some foundational concepts.

Population vs. Sample

Population: The entire group of individuals or instances that you are interested in studying.

Sample: A subset of the population selected for analysis.

For example, we surveyed all the data scientists in the world. Out of those, we randomly selected 500 from various countries to include in the study.

Parameters vs. Statistics

Parameter: A numerical characteristic of a population (e.g., population mean μ\muμ, population standard deviation σ\sigmaσ).

Statistic: A numerical characteristic of a sample (e.g., sample mean x¯\bar{x}x¯, sample standard deviation sss).

Random Variables

A **random variable** is a variable whose possible values are numerical outcomes of a random phenomenon. They are either:

- **Discrete Random Variable**: Takes on countable values (e.g., number of defective items in a batch).
- **Continuous Random Variable**: Takes on an infinite number of possible values within a range (e.g., height, weight).

Probability Distributions

A probability distribution describes how the probabilities are distributed over the values of the random variable. It can be:

- **Discrete Probability Distribution**: Defined by a probability mass function (PMF).
- **Continuous Probability Distribution**: Defined by a probability density function (PDF).

Hypothesis Testing

Hypothesis testing is a formal statistical method used to evaluate assumptions or claims about a population parameter based on sample data. It provides a systematic framework for making decisions about the validity of a hypothesis.

Hypothesis Testing Process

Formulate the Hypotheses

The null hypothesis ($H0$) is the default assumption or status quo (e.g., there is no difference between groups).

The alternative hypothesis (Ha) is the claim or effect we want to test (e.g., there is a difference between groups).

Select a Significance Level

The most common choices are 0.05, 0.01, or 0.10. This shows the probability of rejecting the null hypothesis when it is actually true (type I error).

Choose Appropriate Test Statistic

It really depends on the data type, distribution, sample size, and whether the data meets certain assumptions. There are a few different tests you can use, like the t-test, z-test, and chi-square test.

Compute Test Statistic and P-value

- **Test statistic**: This is a standardized value that's calculated from the data in the sample.
- **P-value**: This is the probability of seeing a test statistic as extreme as, or more extreme than, the value that's been calculated from the sample data. This is done under the assumption that the null hypothesis is true.

Make a Decision

- If P-value$\leq\alpha$, reject the null hypothesis ($H0$).
- If P-value$>\alpha$, fail to reject the null hypothesis.

And then finally, we take a look at the results, which give us some background and tell us what this all means in real-life terms.

Sample Program: Comparing Salaries

Suppose we want to test if the average salary of data analysts is different from that of data scientists.

- **Null Hypothesis ($H0$)**: μAnalysts=μScientists
- **Alternative Hypothesis (Ha)**: μAnalysts$\neq\mu$Scientists

Now, we will perform a two-sample t-test.

Performing Hypothesis Testing

First, we need to load and preprocess the dataset, **ds_salaries.csv**, having the following columns:

- **job_title**: Job title of the individual.
- **salary_in_usd**: Salary in USD.

Following is the quick code snippet:

```
use csv::ReaderBuilder;
use std::error::Error;
#[derive(Debug)]
struct SalaryRecord {
    job_title: String,
    salary_in_usd: f64,
}
fn load_salaries() -> Result<(Vec<f64>, Vec<f64>), Box<dyn
Error>> {
    let mut rdr = ReaderBuilder::new()
        .has_headers(true)
        .from_path("ds_salaries.csv")?;

    let mut data_analysts = Vec::new();
    let mut data_scientists = Vec::new();
    for result in rdr.deserialize() {
        let record: SalaryRecord = result?;
        match record.job_title.as_str() {
            "Data Analyst" =>
data_analysts.push(record.salary_in_usd),
            "Data Scientist" =>
data_scientists.push(record.salary_in_usd),
            _ => (),
        }
    }
    Ok((data_analysts, data_scientists))
}
```

The two-sample t-test compares two sets of data to figure out if there's a statistical difference between them.

Here's where we make our assumptions:

- The data is normally distributed.
- The two groups have the same standard deviation (homoscedasticity).
- The samples are independent.

Next, we'll calculate the test statistic and p-value.

```
use statrs::statistics::{Data, Statistics};
use statrs::distribution::{StudentsT, Continuous};
fn t_test_independent(sample1: &[f64], sample2: &[f64]) ->
(f64, f64, f64) {
    let n1 = sample1.len() as f64;
    let n2 = sample2.len() as f64;
    let mean1 = sample1.mean();
    let mean2 = sample2.mean();
    let var1 = sample1.variance();
    let var2 = sample2.variance();
    // Check for equal variances using F-test (optional)
    let f_stat = var1 / var2;
    // Degrees of freedom for F-test
    let df1 = n1 - 1.0;
    let df2 = n2 - 1.0;
    // We can perform an F-test here if necessary
    // Pooled standard deviation
    let pooled_std = (((n1 - 1.0) * var1 + (n2 - 1.0) * var2)
/ (n1 + n2 - 2.0)).sqrt();
    // Test statistic
    let t_stat = (mean1 - mean2) / (pooled_std * (1.0 / n1 +
1.0 / n2).sqrt());
    // Degrees of freedom
    let df = n1 + n2 - 2.0;
    // P-value
```

```
    let dist = StudentsT::new(0.0, 1.0, df).unwrap();
    let p_value = 2.0 * (1.0 - dist.cdf(t_stat.abs()));
    (t_stat, df, p_value)
}
```

Now we are executing the test:

```
fn main() -> Result<(), Box<dyn Error>> {
    let (data_analysts_salaries, data_scientists_salaries) =
load_salaries()?;
    // Ensure neither sample is empty
    if data_analysts_salaries.is_empty() ||
data_scientists_salaries.is_empty() {
        println!("One of the samples is empty. Cannot perform
t-test.");
        return Ok(());
    }
    let (t_stat, df, p_value) =
t_test_independent(&data_analysts_salaries,
&data_scientists_salaries);
    println!("Two-sample T-test Results:");
    println!("Degrees of Freedom: {:.2}", df);
    println!("T-statistic: {:.4}", t_stat);
    println!("P-value: {:.4}", p_value);
    let alpha = 0.05;
    if p_value < alpha {
        println!("Reject the null hypothesis: There is a
significant difference between the average salaries.");
    } else {
        println!("Fail to reject the null hypothesis: No
significant difference detected.");
    }
    Ok(())
```

```
}
```

Now, how to Make sense of the findings:

- **Reject *H0***: If the p-value is less than the significance level (α/α), we have enough evidence to say there's a real difference in the average salaries.
- **Fail to Reject *H0***: If the p-value is greater than α, we don't have enough evidence to say there's a real difference.

Chi-Square Test for Independence

The chi-square test for independence assesses whether there's a significant association between two categorical variables. Suppose we want to test if the job title (e.g., Data Analyst, Data Scientist, Data Engineer) is independent of the experience level (e.g., Junior, Mid, Senior).

First, we need to create a contingency table from the dataset.

```
use std::collections::HashMap;
#[derive(Debug)]
struct EmployeeRecord {
    job_title: String,
    experience_level: String,
}
fn load_contingency_table() -> Result<HashMap<(String,
String), usize>, Box<dyn Error>> {
    let mut rdr = ReaderBuilder::new()
        .has_headers(true)
        .from_path("ds_salaries.csv")?;

    let mut contingency_table = HashMap::new();
    for result in rdr.deserialize() {
        let record: EmployeeRecord = result?;
        *contingency_table.entry((record.job_title,
record.experience_level)).or_insert(0) += 1;
    }
```

```
    Ok(contingency_table)
}
```

Now, implementing the chi-square test:

```
use statrs::distribution::{ChiSquared, Continuous};

fn chi_square_test(contingency_table: &HashMap<(String,
String), usize>) -> (f64, f64) {

    // Extract unique job titles and experience levels

    let job_titles: Vec<_> =
contingency_table.keys().map(|(job, _)|
job.clone()).collect();

    let experience_levels: Vec<_> =
contingency_table.keys().map(|(_, exp)|
exp.clone()).collect();

    let unique_job_titles: Vec<_> =
job_titles.iter().cloned().collect::<std::collections::HashSet
<_>>().into_iter().collect();

    let unique_experience_levels: Vec<_> =
experience_levels.iter().cloned().collect::<std::collections::
HashSet<_>>().into_iter().collect();

    let mut observed = Vec::new();

    let mut expected = Vec::new();

    let total_count: usize = contingency_table.values().sum();

    for job in &unique_job_titles {

        for exp in &unique_experience_levels {

            let observed_count =
*contingency_table.get(&(job.clone(),
exp.clone())).unwrap_or(&0);

            observed.push(observed_count as f64);

            // Calculate marginal totals

            let row_total: usize =
unique_experience_levels.iter()
```

```
                .map(|e| *contingency_table.get(&(job.clone(),
e.clone())).unwrap_or(&0))
                .sum();
            let column_total: usize = unique_job_titles.iter()
                .map(|j| *contingency_table.get(&(j.clone(),
exp.clone())).unwrap_or(&0))
                .sum();
            let expected_count = (row_total as f64) *
(column_total as f64) / (total_count as f64);
            expected.push(expected_count);
        }
    }
    // Calculate chi-square statistic
    let chi_square_stat =
observed.iter().zip(expected.iter()).map(|(o, e)| {
        if *e != 0.0 {
            (*o - *e).powi(2) / *e
        } else {
            0.0
        }
    }).sum::<f64>();
    // Degrees of freedom
    let df = (unique_job_titles.len() - 1) *
(unique_experience_levels.len() - 1);
    // P-value
    let dist = ChiSquared::new(df as f64).unwrap();
    let p_value = 1.0 - dist.cdf(chi_square_stat);
    (chi_square_stat, p_value)
}
```

Next, executing the test:

```
fn main() -> Result<(), Box<dyn Error>> {
    let contingency_table = load_contingency_table()?;
    let (chi_square_stat, p_value) =
chi_square_test(&contingency_table);
    println!("Chi-Square Test for Independence:");
    println!("Chi-Square Statistic: {:.4}", chi_square_stat);
    println!("P-value: {:.4}", p_value);
    let alpha = 0.05;
    if p_value < alpha {
        println!("Reject the null hypothesis: There is an
association between job title and experience level.");
    } else {
        println!("Fail to reject the null hypothesis: No
significant association detected.");
    }
    Ok(())
}
```

Now, let's look at the results. We can reject $H0$, which means there's a significant link between job title and experience level. Otherwise, we can't reject $H0$, which means there's no significant link between the variables and they're basically independent.

Confidence Intervals

Confidence intervals show us a range of possible values for a population parameter, like the mean or proportion. They help us understand how likely it is that the true value of the parameter will fall within that range, for example, 95% of the time. Confidence intervals help data scientists and statisticians to quantify the precision of their estimates by showing how uncertain the point estimates really are.

For example, if a data scientist is estimating the average salary of data analysts, they might compute a 95% confidence interval. This would show that they're 95% confident that the true average salary falls within the specified range. This info can be useful when it comes to making decisions and allocating resources, as it gives an idea of how sure we can be about the estimates.

Confidence Interval for Mean

For a sample mean $\bar{x}$ and known standard deviation 's':

$$CI = \bar{x} \pm t^{*} \left(\frac{s}{\sqrt{n}} \right)$$

- t^*: Critical value from the t-distribution.
- n: Sample size.

Given below is a simple implementation example using the same function **confidence_interval_mean** from earlier. Here, we calculate a 95% confidence interval for the average salary of data analysts.

```
fn main() -> Result<(), Box<dyn Error>> {
    let (data_analysts_salaries, _) = load_salaries()?;
    let confidence_level = 0.95;
    let (lower_bound, upper_bound) =
confidence_interval_mean(&data_analysts_salaries,
confidence_level);
    println!("{}% Confidence Interval for Data Analysts' Mean
Salary:", confidence_level * 100.0);
    println!("Lower Bound: {:.2}", lower_bound);
    println!("Upper Bound: {:.2}", upper_bound);
    Ok(())
}
```

Confidence Interval for Proportion

For a sample proportion p^\hat{p}p^:

$$CI - \hat{p} \pm z^{*} \sqrt{\frac{\hat{p}(1-\hat{p})}{n}}$$

Here, z^* is the critical value from the standard normal distribution.

Now suppose we want to calculate the confidence interval for the proportion of data scientists who work remotely.

```
#[derive(Debug)]
struct RemoteRecord {
    job_title: String,
    remote_ratio: u8, // 0 for no remote, 50 for partially
remote, 100 for fully remote
}
fn load_remote_ratios() -> Result<Vec<f64>, Box<dyn Error>> {
    let mut rdr = ReaderBuilder::new()
        .has_headers(true)
        .from_path("ds_salaries.csv")?;

    let mut remote_ratios = Vec::new();
    for result in rdr.deserialize() {
        let record: RemoteRecord = result?;
        if record.job_title == "Data Scientist" {
            if record.remote_ratio > 0 {
                remote_ratios.push(1.0); // Consider any
remote work as 'remote'
            } else {
                remote_ratios.push(0.0);
            }
        }
    }
    Ok(remote_ratios)
}
```

We can use the confidence_interval_proportion function from earlier to calculate the confidence interval.

```
fn main() -> Result<(), Box<dyn Error>> {
```

```
    let remote_ratios = load_remote_ratios()?;
    let confidence_level = 0.95;
    let (lower_bound, upper_bound) =
confidence_interval_proportion(&remote_ratios,
confidence_level);
    println!("{}% Confidence Interval for Proportion of Data
Scientists Working Remotely:", confidence_level * 100.0);
    println!("Lower Bound: {:.4}", lower_bound);
    println!("Upper Bound: {:.4}", upper_bound);
    Ok(())
}
```

From what we can see, we can say with about 95% certainty that the actual number of data scientists working remotely is somewhere within the calculated range.

Parametric Tests

Parametric tests are a category of statistical tests that operate under specific assumptions about the data being analyzed. These assumptions often involve the data following a normal distribution and having equal variances across groups. When these conditions are met, parametric tests tend to be more powerful and accurate than non-parametric alternatives.

Some widely-used parametric tests are:

- **T-test**: Utilized for comparing the means of two groups, the t-test assumes that the data is normally distributed and that variances are equal between the groups.
- **ANOVA (Analysis of Variance)**: ANOVA is employed for comparing the means of three or more groups, making the same assumptions as the t-test regarding normality and equal variances.
- **Linear regression**: A technique for modeling the relationship between a dependent variable and one or more independent variables, linear regression assumes that the residuals (errors) follow a normal distribution and that the relationship between variables is linear.

When the assumptions underlying parametric tests hold true, these tests can provide more accurate and reliable results. However, it is essential to carefully examine the data and validate the assumptions before applying parametric tests to avoid inaccurate conclusions.

In this section, we'll describe and perform the following parametric tests on the given database:

1. Paired T-test
2. One-way ANOVA

Paired T-Test

A paired t-test compares two related samples, such as measurements before and after a treatment on the same subjects.

In our dataset, we don't have paired data, but we can create a hypothetical scenario where we compare the salaries of data analysts and data scientists working in the same company. For simplicity, let's assume that both groups have the same number of employees.

```
fn paired_t_test(sample1: &[f64], sample2: &[f64]) -> (f64,
f64, f64) {
    let differences: Vec<f64> =
sample1.iter().zip(sample2).map(|(x, y)| x - y).collect();
    let n = differences.len() as f64;
    let mean_diff = differences.mean();
    let std_diff = differences.std_dev();
    let t_stat = mean_diff / (std_diff / n.sqrt());
    let df = n - 1.0;
    let dist = StudentsT::new(0.0, 1.0, df).unwrap();
    let p_value = 2.0 * (1.0 - dist.cdf(t_stat.abs()));
    (t_stat, df, p_value)
}
```

Do not forgete to ensure that both **sample1** and **sample2** are of the same length and correspond to the same subjects.

One-Way ANOVA

A one-way ANOVA is used to compare the means of three or more independent groups to determine if there is a significant difference between them. In the below sample program, let's compare the mean salaries of data analysts, data scientists, and data engineers.

Now here, we will use statrs crate just to get well versed with another prominent package of Rust:

```
use statrs::function::factorial::ln_gamma;
```

```
use statrs::function::traits::Exp;
fn f_distribution_quantile(df1: f64, df2: f64, alpha: f64) ->
f64 {
    let x = (df2 / (df1 * (1.0 - alpha).ln().exp() +
df2)).ln().exp();
    x / (1.0 + x)
}
fn one_way_anova(groups: &[Array1<f64>], alpha: f64) -> (f64,
f64) {
    let k = groups.len() as f64;
    let n_total: f64 = groups.iter().map(|g| g.len() as
f64).sum();
let grand_mean = groups.iter().map(|g| g.sum()).sum::<f64>() /
n_total;
let ss_between: f64 = groups
    .iter()
    .map(|g| {
        let group_mean = g.mean().unwrap();
        let group_size = g.len() as f64;
        group_size * (group_mean - grand_mean).powi(2)
    })
    .sum();
let ss_within: f64 = groups
    .iter()
    .map(|g| g.mapv(|x| (x -
g.mean().unwrap()).powi(2)).sum())
    .sum();
let df_between = k - 1.0;
let df_within = n_total - k;
let ms_between = ss_between / df_between;
let ms_within = ss_within / df_within;
```

```
let f_stat = ms_between / ms_within;
let f_alpha = f_distribution_quantile(df_between, df_within,
1.0 - alpha);
(f_stat, f_alpha)
}
fn main() {
// Assume data_analysts_salaries, data_scientists_salaries,
and data_engineers_salaries are already loaded.
let alpha = 0.05;
let (f_stat, f_alpha) = one_way_anova(
    &[
        data_analysts_salaries.clone(),
        data_scientists_salaries.clone(),
        data_engineers_salaries.clone(),
    ],
    alpha,
);
println!("One-way ANOVA (1 - α = {:.2}):", 1.0 - alpha);
println!("F-statistic: {:.4}", f_stat);
println!("Critical value: {:.4}", f_alpha);
if f_stat > f_alpha {
    println!("There is a significant difference between the
groups.");
} else {
    println!("There is no significant difference between the
groups.");
}
}
```

In the above sample program, we perform a one-way ANOVA test on the salaries of data analysts, data scientists, and data engineers using the statrs package. The test produces an F-statistic, which we compare against the critical value obtained from the F-distribution. If the F-statistic is greater than the critical value, we can conclude that there is a significant difference between the mean salaries of the groups.

Non-Parametric Tests

Non-parametric tests are a category of statistical tests that refrain from making assumptions about the underlying data distribution. These tests prove valuable when the data does not meet the prerequisites of parametric tests, such as normality, equal variances, or homoscedasticity. As a result, non-parametric tests are more robust and applicable to a broader range of data types, including ordinal and non-normally distributed data.

Several popular non-parametric tests are widely used in various research fields. The Wilcoxon rank-sum test (also known as the Mann-Whitney U test) is employed to compare two independent samples without assuming normality. The Kruskal-Wallis test extends this concept to handle more than two groups, serving as a non-parametric alternative to the parametric one-way analysis of variance (ANOVA). Lastly, Spearman's rank correlation is a technique that assesses the strength and direction of a monotonic relationship between two variables, without requiring a linear relationship or normally distributed data.

Here, we'll describe and perform the following non-parametric tests on the given database:

- Wilcoxon rank-sum test (Mann-Whitney U test)
- Kruskal-Wallis test

Wilcoxon Rank-Sum Test (Mann-Whitney U Test)

The Wilcoxon rank-sum test, alternatively referred to as the Mann-Whitney U test, is a non-parametric statistical test employed to assess whether two independent samples have significantly different distributions. This test is particularly useful when dealing with non-normally distributed data or when the sample sizes are small, as it makes no assumptions about the underlying population distributions.

The test works by ranking the combined data from both samples and then summing the ranks within each sample. The rank-sums are then compared to evaluate if there is a significant difference between the distributions. The Mann-Whitney U statistic is computed from these rank-sums, and its distribution under the null hypothesis is used to calculate the p-value. If the p-value is below a predetermined significance level (typically 0.05), the null hypothesis that both samples originate from the same distribution is rejected, suggesting a significant difference between the two distributions. In contrast, if the p-value is above the threshold, there is insufficient evidence to reject the null hypothesis, and no significant difference between the distributions can be claimed. By applying the Wilcoxon rank-sum test, researchers can effectively determine whether two independent samples differ significantly in terms of their distributions.

Let's compare the salary distributions of data analysts and data scientists.

```
use ndarray_stats::QuantileExt;
use statrs::function::erf::erf;
use statrs::function::traits::Exp;
fn wilcoxon_rank_sum_test(sample1: &Array1<f64>, sample2:
&Array1<f64>, alpha: f64) -> bool {
    let combined =
sample1.clone().into_iter().chain(sample2.clone().into_iter())
.collect::<Vec<_>>();
    let ranks =
ndarray_stats::sort::argsort(&Array1::from(combined.clone())).
into_iter().map(|&i| i as f64 + 1.0).collect::<Vec<_>>();
    let rank_sum1 = sample1.len() as f64 * (sample1.len() + 1)
as f64 / 2.0;
    let rank_sum2: f64 =
ranks.iter().take(sample1.len()).sum();
    let u = rank_sum1 - rank_sum2;
    let n1 = sample1.len() as f64;
    let n2 = sample2.len() as f64;
    let mu = n1 * n2 / 2.0;
    let sigma = ((n1 * n2 * (n1 + n2 + 1)) / 12.0).sqrt();
    let z = (u - mu) / sigma;
    let p_value = 2.0 * (1.0 - 0.5 * (1.0 + erf(-z.abs() /
2.0f64.sqrt())));
    p_value < alpha
}
fn main() {
    // Assume data_analysts_salaries and
data_scientists_salaries are already loaded.
    let alpha = 0.05;
    let significant =
wilcoxon_rank_sum_test(&data_analysts_salaries,
&data_scientists_salaries, alpha);
```

```
    println!("Wilcoxon rank-sum test (α = {:.2}):", alpha);
    println!("Is there a significant difference? {}",
significant);
}
```

In the above sample program, we calculated the p-value for the Wilcoxon rank-sum test comparing the salary distributions of data analysts and data scientists. If the p-value is less than the significance level (alpha), it suggests that there is a significant difference between the two distributions.

Kruskal-Wallis Test

The Kruskal-Wallis test serves as a non-parametric alternative to the one-way ANOVA when the assumptions of normality and homogeneity of variances are not met. It is employed to compare the distributions of three or more independent samples, assessing whether there is a statistically significant difference among them. Instead of relying on the means, as in the one-way ANOVA, the Kruskal-Wallis test focuses on the median and rankings of the data points. It ranks the data from all samples combined and calculates the sum of ranks for each group. The test statistic, H, is then computed based on these rank sums and compared to a chi-square distribution with (k-1) degrees of freedom, where k represents the number of groups.

If the calculated H statistic is greater than the critical chi-square value, the null hypothesis, which assumes that all samples come from the same distribution, is rejected. This indicates a significant difference among the sample distributions. The Kruskal-Wallis test is a valuable tool in cases where parametric assumptions are not satisfied, enabling robust analysis of the differences between multiple independent samples.

Let us compare the salary distributions of data analysts, data scientists, and data engineers.

```
fn kruskal_wallis(groups: &[Array
1<f64>], alpha: f64) -> bool {
let n_total = groups.iter().map(|g| g.len() as f64).sum();
let k = groups.len() as f64;
let mut combined = groups
    .iter()
    .enumerate()
    .flat_map(|(i, g)| g.iter().map(move |&x| (i, x)))
    .collect::<Vec<_>>();
```

```
combined.sort_unstable_by(|(_, a), (_, b)|
a.partial_cmp(b).unwrap());
let ranks = combined
    .iter()
    .enumerate()
    .map(|(i, (group, _))| (*group, i as f64 + 1.0))
    .collect::<Vec<_>>();
let rank_sums: Vec<f64> = (0..groups.len())
    .map(|i| {
        ranks
            .iter()
            .filter(|(group, _)| *group == i)
            .map(|(_, rank)| rank)
            .sum::<f64>()
    })
    .collect();
let h_stat = 12.0
    / (n_total * (n_total + 1.0))
    * rank_sums
        .iter()
        .enumerate()
        .map(|(i, &r)| r.powi(2) / groups[i].len() as f64)
        .sum::<f64>()
    - 3.0 * (n_total + 1.0);
let chi2_alpha = statrs::distribution::ChiSquared::new(k -
1.0).unwrap().inverse_cdf(1.0 - alpha);
h_stat > chi2_alpha
}
fn main() {
```

```
// Assume data_analysts_salaries, data_scientists_salaries,
and data_engineers_salaries are already loaded.
let alpha = 0.05;
let significant = kruskal_wallis(
    &[
        data_analysts_salaries.clone(),
        data_scientists_salaries.clone(),
        data_engineers_salaries.clone(),
    ],
    alpha,
);
println!("Kruskal-Wallis test (α = {:.2}):", alpha);
println!("Is there a significant difference? {}",
significant);
}
```

In the above sample program, we calculate the H-statistic for the Kruskal-Wallis test comparing the salary distributions of data analysts, data scientists, and data engineers. If the H-statistic is greater than the critical value obtained from the Chi-squared distribution, it suggests that there is a significant difference between the three distributions.

Summary

You should now have a much better grasp of statistical hypothesis testing. A variety of tests, such as chi-square tests and analysis of variance (ANOVA), were implemented to compare groups and evaluate the relationships that exist within the data. With this chapter, you can now choose the right tests to run depending on the assumptions and features of your data.

Additionally, you gained the ability to interpret p-values and significance levels, gaining an understanding of the implications these measurements have for accepting or rejecting hypothesis. You improved your capacity to carry out reliable statistical analyses by acknowledging the possibility of making mistakes and the significance of the assumptions required for testing. This set of abilities is absolutely necessary for research, data science, and any other field that requires conclusions that are supported by evidence.

CHAPTER 6: REGRESSION ANALYSIS

Overview

The topic of time series analysis, which focuses on data collected over time intervals, is presented to you in this chapter. Seasonality, cyclical patterns, and trends are some of the time series data components that you will examine in this chapter. You will learn to visualize and decompose time series data using ndarray and ndarray-stats crates. This will help you uncover underlying structures.

A number of different forecasting methods, including moving averages, exponential smoothing, and ARIMA models, are learned in this chapter. You will be able to use these techniques to make value predictions using past data. You will learn the skills necessary to evaluate time series data and generate accurate predictions at the conclusion of this chapter. These abilities are vital in fields such as economics and finance.

Introduction to Regression Analysis

Overview

Regression analysis is a powerful statistical technique that helps us understand the relationship between one thing (the "dependent variable") and one or more things that might have caused it ("independent variables"). It's a core tool in data science because it lets professionals model and grasp how complex variables relate to one another, make predictions, and identify what's really driving outcomes.

What's great about regression analysis is that it helps researchers, analysts, and decision-makers get meaningful insights from data. It's a structured way to quantify relationships between variables, which makes it easier to understand and communicate the results. By grasping these relationships, professionals can make better-informed decisions, optimize processes, and develop strategies to achieve specific goals.

Applications of Regression Analysis

At its core, regression analysis allows us to:

Some of the breakthroughs that regression analysis has brought to statistical problems include:

- **Predictive Modeling**: Regression analysis is widely used to develop predictive models that estimate the value of a dependent variable based on the values of the independent variables. These models can help businesses forecast sales, predict customer churn, estimate housing prices, and optimize marketing campaigns, among other applications.
- **Causality Analysis**: While correlation does not imply causation, regression analysis can provide evidence of causality by controlling for potential confounding factors. This helps researchers determine whether an observed relationship between variables is causal or merely coincidental, leading to better decision-making and policy development.

- **Variable Selection**: Regression analysis can be used to identify the most important independent variables that influence a dependent variable. This helps researchers and analysts focus on the key factors that drive outcomes, leading to more efficient resource allocation and targeted interventions.
- **Interaction Effects**: Regression analysis can model interaction effects between independent variables, which can reveal complex relationships that would be difficult to detect otherwise. This can lead to a deeper understanding of how different factors work together to impact outcomes.

Regression models are invaluable tools in various domains, including economics, engineering, social sciences, and natural sciences. They help professionals make informed decisions by providing insights derived from data.

Types of Regression Analysis

There are several types of regression analysis, each suited to specific types of data and research questions:

- **Linear Regression**: Linear regression is the simplest form of regression analysis, which models the relationship between a dependent variable and one or more independent variables as a straight line. It assumes that the relationship between the variables is linear, and the errors are normally distributed, independent, and have constant variance.
- **Multiple Regression**: Multiple regression is an extension of linear regression that incorporates multiple independent variables. It allows for a more complex representation of the relationships between variables and can account for potential confounding factors.
- **Polynomial Regression**: Polynomial regression is a form of linear regression that models the relationship between the dependent variable and the independent variables as a polynomial function. It can capture non-linear relationships in the data but may be prone to overfitting.
- **Logistic Regression**: Logistic regression is used when the dependent variable is binary or categorical. It models the probability of an event occurring, such as a customer making a urchase or a patient developing a specific disease.
- **Ridge and Lasso Regression**: Ridge and Lasso regression are techniques used to address multicollinearity, overfitting, and high-dimensional data in linear regression. They introduce regularization terms that penalize large coefficients, leading to more stable and interpretable models.
- **Non-linear Regression**: Non-linear regression models complex relationships between variables that cannot be captured by linear or polynomial regression. It requires more advanced techniques, such as neural networks or decision trees, to fit the data.

Knowing about these different regression techniques helps data scientists choose the best model for their data and research goals. And thanks to all the different types and uses of regression analysis, it's brought some big changes to statistics. Researchers and analysts can use it to get meaningful insights from data, make informed choices and develop effective strategies.

Simple Linear Regression

Understanding Equation

Simple linear regression is a statistical method that models the relationship between a dependent variable (response) and a single independent variable (predictor). The relationship between the two variables is assumed to be linear, meaning that a change in the independent variable corresponds to a proportional change in the dependent variable. The model takes the form:

$$y = \beta_0 + \beta_1 x + \epsilon$$

where y is the dependent variable, x is the independent variable, β_0 is the intercept, $\beta_1$is the slope, and ε is the random error term.

The goal of simple linear regression is to find the best-fitting line through the data points. To achieve this, we aim to minimize the sum of squared residuals (the differences between the observed and predicted values). This is known as the method of least squares.

Applying Simple Regression

So here now, let us now aim to model the relationship between **salary_in_usd** (dependent variable) and **work_year** (independent variable).

At first, add the following dependencies to your **Cargo.toml**:

```
[dependencies]
csv = "1.1"
ndarray = "0.15"
ndarray-stats = "0.4"
ndarray-linalg = { version = "0.15", features = ["openblas-
static"] }
plotters = "0.3" # Optional for visualization
```

Next, we'll go over loading and preparing data:

```
use csv::ReaderBuilder;
use ndarray::Array1;
use std::error::Error;
fn load_data() -> Result<(Array1<f64>, Array1<f64>), Box<dyn
Error>> {
    let mut rdr = ReaderBuilder::new()
        .has_headers(true)
        .from_path("ds_salaries.csv")?;
    let mut work_year = Vec::new();
    let mut salary_in_usd = Vec::new();
    for result in rdr.records() {
        let record = result?;
        let year: f64 = record.get(0).unwrap().parse()?;
        let salary: f64 = record.get(4).unwrap().parse()?;
        work_year.push(year);
        salary_in_usd.push(salary);
    }
    Ok((
        Array1::from(work_year),
        Array1::from(salary_in_usd),
    ))
}
```

Let's walk through implementing simple linear regression.

```
use ndarray::prelude::*;
use ndarray_stats::CorrelationExt;
fn simple_linear_regression(x: &Array1<f64>, y: &Array1<f64>)
-> (f64, f64) {
    let n = x.len() as f64;
    let x_mean = x.mean().unwrap();
```

```
    let y_mean = y.mean().unwrap();
    let numerator = (x - x_mean).dot(&(y - y_mean));
    let denominator = (x - x_mean).mapv(|a| a.powi(2)).sum();
    let beta1 = numerator / denominator;
    let beta0 = y_mean - beta1 * x_mean;
    (beta0, beta1)
}
fn main() -> Result<(), Box<dyn Error>> {
    let (work_year, salary_in_usd) = load_data()?;
    let (beta0, beta1) = simple_linear_regression(&work_year,
&salary_in_usd);
    println!("Intercept (β0): {:.2}", beta0);
    println!("Slope (β1): {:.2}", beta1);
    // Predict salary for specific work years
    let test_years = array![5.0, 10.0, 15.0];
    let predicted_salaries = &beta0 + &beta1 * &test_years;
    println!("Predicted Salaries: {:?}", predicted_salaries);
    Ok(())
}
```

Now let us look at the results. Consider that the output is:

```
Intercept (β0): 40000.00
Slope (β1): 3000.00
Predicted Salaries: [55000.0, 70000.0, 85000.0]
```

These values are the predicted salaries for employees with 5, 10, and 15 years of work experience, respectively, according to the simple linear regression model.

When **work_year** is 0, the expected **salary_in_usd** is $40,000. For each additional year of work experience, the salary increases by $3,000. The predictions can be that an employee with 5 years of experience is predicted probably to earn $55,000.

Multiple Linear Regression

Understanding Equation

Multiple linear regression extends simple linear regression by incorporating multiple independent variables. The model is:

$$y = \beta_0 + \beta_1 x_1 + \beta_2 x_2 + \cdots + \beta_p x_p + \epsilon$$

Here,

- y: Dependent variable.
- $x1, x2, \ldots, x$: Independent variables.
- $\beta 0$: Intercept.
- $\beta 1, \beta 2, \ldots, \beta p$: Coefficients for each independent variable.
- ϵ: Error term.

Applying Multiple Regression

Same as simple linear regression, with additional consideration for Multicollinearity in which independent ariables should not be highly correlated with each other. Now here, let us assume that you want to predict **salary_in_usd** based on **work_year** and **remote_ratio**.

```
fn load_data_multiple() -> Result<(Array2<f64>, Array1<f64>),
Box<dyn Error>> {
    let mut rdr = ReaderBuilder::new()
        .has_headers(true)
        .from_path("ds_salaries.csv")?;
    let mut features = Vec::new();
    let mut salary_in_usd = Vec::new();
    for result in rdr.records() {
        let record = result?;
        let year: f64 = record.get(0).unwrap().parse()?;
        let remote_ratio: f64 =
record.get(8).unwrap().parse()?;
        let salary: f64 = record.get(4).unwrap().parse()?;
```

```
        features.push(vec![year, remote_ratio]);
        salary_in_usd.push(salary);
    }
    Ok((
        Array2::from(features),
        Array1::from(salary_in_usd),
    ))
}
```

We can use the below normal equation to solve for coefficients:

$$\beta = (X^T X)^{-1} X^T y$$

```
use ndarray_linalg::Solve;
fn multiple_linear_regression(X: &Array2<f64>, y:
&Array1<f64>) -> Array1<f64> {
    // Add intercept term
    let ones = Array2::ones((X.nrows(), 1));
    let X_with_intercept = ndarray::concatenate![Axis(1),
ones, X];
    // Compute coefficients
    let xtx = X_with_intercept.t().dot(&X_with_intercept);
    let xty = X_with_intercept.t().dot(y);
    let beta = xtx.solve_into(xty).unwrap();
    beta
}
fn main() -> Result<(), Box<dyn Error>> {
    let (X, y) = load_data_multiple()?;
    let beta = multiple_linear_regression(&X, &y);
    println!("Coefficients: {:?}", beta);
    // Predict for new data
```

```
    let test_data = array![[1.0, 5.0, 0.5], [1.0, 10.0, 0.2],
[1.0, 15.0, 0.8]];
    let y_pred = test_data.dot(&beta);
    println!("Predicted Salaries: {:?}", y_pred);
    Ok(())
}
```

Following is what the output might look like:

```
Intercept: 38000.00
Coefficients: [2950.00, 5000.00]
Predicted salaries: [52500.00, 66500.00, 91000.00]
```

These values are the predicted salaries for employees with the specified combinations of work years and remote ratios, according to the multiple linear regression model.

Overall, we fit a multiple linear regression model to the data. After fitting the model, we print the intercept and coefficients, which represent the estimated values of β0, β1, β2, etc. Then, we make predictions for specific work years and remote ratios using the predict method.

Polynomial Regression

Understanding the Equation

Polynomial regression is a type of regression analysis that models the relationship between a dependent variable and one or more independent variables using a polynomial function. It allows for a more flexible representation of the relationships between variables, capturing non-linear relationships in the data. The polynomial regression model takes the form:

$$y = \beta_0 + \beta_1 x + \beta_2 x^2 + \cdots + \beta_n x^n + \epsilon$$

where y is the dependent variable, x is the independent variable, $\beta 0$ is the intercept, $\beta 1, \beta 2, \dots, \beta n$ are the coefficients for each term, and ε is the random error term.

The goal of polynomial regression is to find the best-fitting curve through the data points, minimizing the sum of squared residuals, similar to linear regression.

Applying Polynomial Regression

Suppose we suspect that the relationship between **work_year** and **salary_in_usd** is non-linear. For this, we need to create additional features representing the polynomial terms.

```
fn generate_polynomial_features(x: &Array1<f64>, degree:
usize) -> Array2<f64> {
    let mut features = Vec::new();
    for i in 0..x.len() {
        let mut row = Vec::new();
        for d in 0..=degree {
            row.push(x[i].powi(d as i32));
        }
        features.push(row);
    }
    Array2::from(features)
}
```

When you're implementing Polynomial Regression, just use the same multiple linear regression approach on the transformed features.

```
fn main() -> Result<(), Box<dyn Error>> {
    let (work_year, salary_in_usd) = load_data()?;
    let degree = 2;
    let X_poly = generate_polynomial_features(&work_year,
degree);
    let beta = multiple_linear_regression(&X_poly.slice(s![..,
1..]), &salary_in_usd);
    println!("Coefficients: {:?}", beta);
    // Predict for new data
    let test_years = array![5.0, 10.0, 15.0];
    let test_X_poly =
generate_polynomial_features(&test_years, degree);
    let y_pred = test_X_poly.slice(s![.., 1..]).dot(&beta);
    println!("Predicted Salaries: {:?}", y_pred);
```

```
    Ok(())
}
```

Suppose the output is:

```
Intercept: 42000.00
Coefficients: [2800.00, -50.00]
Predicted salaries: [55750.00, 72000.00, 88450.00]
```

These values are the predicted salaries for employees with 5, 10, and 15 years of work experience, respectively, according to the second-degree polynomial regression model.

The model captures a non-linear pattern between **work_year** and **salary_in_usd**.

Logistic Regression

Understanding Equation

Logistic regression is a statistical method used for analyzing a dataset in which the dependent variable is binary or categorical (i.e., it has two possible outcomes). It is an extension of linear regression, specifically tailored for predicting binary outcomes by using a logistic function, which outputs probabilities between 0 and 1.

The logistic function, also known as the sigmoid function, is given by:

$$P(y=1|x)=\frac{1}{1+e^{-(\beta_0+\beta_1x_1+\cdots+\beta_px_p)}}$$

Applying Logistic Regression

Suppose we want to predict whether a job is remote based on features.

```
fn load_data_logistic() -> Result<(Array2<f64>, Array1<f64>),
Box<dyn Error>> {
    // Similar to previous, but target is binary
    // For example, remote_ratio > 0 => 1, else 0
}
```

Consider using the **linfa** crate, which provides machine learning algorithms.

Add the following to the Cargo.toml:

```
[dependencies]
linfa = "0.6"
linfa-logistic = "0.6"
ndarray = "0.15"
```

Now, let's implement logistic regression:

```
use linfa::prelude::*;
use linfa_logistic::LogisticRegression;
use ndarray::Array2;
fn main() -> Result<(), Box<dyn Error>> {
    let (X, y) = load_data_logistic()?;
    // Split data into training and testing sets
    let dataset = Dataset::new(X, y);
    let (train, valid) = dataset.split_with_ratio(0.8);
    // Fit the model
    let model = LogisticRegression::default()
        .fit(&train)?;
    // Predict on validation set
    let pred = model.predict(&valid);
    // Evaluate accuracy
    let acc =
pred.confusion_matrix(&valid).unwrap().accuracy();
    println!("Accuracy: {:.2}%", acc * 100.0);
    Ok(())
}
```

Following is what the output might look like:

```
Predicted probability: 0.75
Predicted class: 1
```

These values indicate the predicted probability of the positive outcome (1) for a specific example using logistic regression and the final class prediction.

Summary

After finishing this chapter, you will have acquired skills that are essential in the field of time series analysis. You gained the ability to analyze time series data by breaking it down into its constituent parts and understanding their patterns. You improved your capacity to understand seasonality and temporal trends by visualizing data with Rust.

With the help of Rust, you were able to implement forecasting models such as moving averages and ARIMA, which gave you the ability to make predictions based on data that is dependent on time. You improved your ability to analyze temporal data by connecting theoretical concepts to practical applications through hands-on coding, which helped you strengthen your proficiency in this area. These are skills that are absolutely necessary for working in fields that rely on accurate forecasting and trend analysis.

CHAPTER 7: BAYESIAN STATISTICS

Overview

In this chapter, you will begin with machine learning, gaining an understanding of its core basics as well as its various applications. You will study both supervised and unsupervised learning paradigms, with a particular emphasis on algorithms such as linear classifiers, k-nearest neighbors (KNN), and k-means clustering techniques. You will implement these algorithms on real datasets by making use of the smartcore and linfa crates.

Methods of model evaluation and validation, such as confusion matrices and cross-validation, are emphasized throughout this chapter. It will be taught to you how to evaluate the performance of a model and how to avoid common pitfalls such as overfitting. Your knowledge of basic machine learning concepts and your ability to apply models will be solidified by the time you finish this chapter.

Introduction to Bayesian Statistics

Overview

Bayesian statistics is a paradigm within the field of statistics that provides a robust mathematical framework for updating beliefs in the presence of new evidence. Named after Reverend Thomas Bayes, an 18th-century mathematician and theologian, Bayesian statistics fundamentally revolves around the concept of updating prior beliefs using Bayes' theorem. This approach contrasts with the frequentist perspective, which relies solely on the frequency or proportion of data without incorporating prior beliefs.

In Bayesian statistics, all forms of uncertainty are expressed in terms of probability distributions. These probabilities are subjective and represent a degree of belief or confidence in a particular event or hypothesis. By continually updating these probabilities as new data becomes available, Bayesian methods offer a dynamic and intuitive way to model real-world phenomena.

Bayes' Theorem

The main idea behind Bayesian statistics is to update the probability of a hypothesis or an event based on the available data and our prior knowledge. This is done using Bayes' theorem, which states that the posterior probability of a hypothesis (the probability after observing the data) is proportional to the product of the likelihood (how likely the data is under the hypothesis) and the prior probability (our initial belief about the hypothesis).

Bayes' theorem can be expressed as:

$$P(H|D) = \frac{P(D|H) \cdot P(H)}{P(D)}$$

Where:

- $P(H \mid D)P(H \mid D)P(H \mid D)$ is the **posterior probability**: the probability of the hypothesis H after observing data D.
- $P(D \mid H)P(D \mid H)P(D \mid H)$ is the **likelihood**: the probability of observing data D given that hypothesis H is true.
- $P(H)P(H)P(H)$ is the **prior probability**: the initial probability of the hypothesis H before observing data D.
- $P(D)P(D)P(D)$ is the **evidence** or **marginal likelihood**: the total probability of observing data D under all possible hypotheses.

The mathematical rule provided by Bayes' theorem allows us to update our belief in a hypothesis based on new evidence. It combines prior knowledge with new data, thereby producing a revised probability, the posterior probability.

Advantages of Bayesian Statistics

Bayesian statistics offers several key advantages over traditional frequentist methods:

- **Incorporation of prior knowledge**: Bayesian statistics allows us to incorporate our prior beliefs or expert knowledge into our analysis. This can be especially valuable in situations where data is scarce, or when we have reason to believe that certain outcomes are more likely than others.
- **Handling uncertainty**: Bayesian statistics provides a natural framework for dealing with uncertainty. In Bayesian analysis, we always work with probabilities, and we can incorporate uncertainties about parameters and models in a principled way. This is in contrast to frequentist statistics, where uncertainty is often expressed using confidence intervals, which can be more difficult to interpret.
- **Model comparison and selection**: Bayesian statistics offers a systematic way of comparing and selecting models, based on their ability to explain the observed data. This can be done using methods such as the Bayes factor, which compares the evidence for two competing models. Bayesian model comparison can help us choose between different hypotheses or explanations for the data.
- **Hierarchical modeling**: Bayesian statistics is well-suited for hierarchical modeling, which is a technique for modeling complex data structures by incorporating multiple levels of dependency. Hierarchical models can be used to capture the structure of data and to share

information across different levels of the hierarchy, resulting in more efficient and accurate estimates.

- **Sequential updating**: Bayesian analysis can be easily updated with new data. As we observe new data, we can update our posterior probabilities and refine our beliefs about the underlying parameters or hypotheses. This is a powerful feature of Bayesian statistics, as it allows for real-time updating and learning from data.
- **Flexibility**: Bayesian methods can be applied to a wide range of statistical problems and models, including linear regression, generalized linear models, time series analysis, and many others. Bayesian methods are also well-suited for working with complex data structures, such as networks or high-dimensional data.

By embracing the Bayesian paradigm, analysts and researchers can build models that are both flexible and reflective of prior knowledge, leading to more robust and interpretable results.

Bayesian Inference

Understanding Bayesian Inference

Bayesian inference allows us to update our beliefs about unknown parameters or hypotheses using the framework of Bayesian statistics. This is based on observed data. It relies on Bayes' theorem, which is the foundation for computing the posterior probability. This represents our updated beliefs after observing the data, combining our prior knowledge or beliefs with the likelihood of the observed data. In short, Bayesian inference is the method we use to draw conclusions about unknown quantities based on observed data and our prior beliefs.

The given below is how Bayesian inference works in the context of Bayesian statistics:

- **Prior probability**: We start by defining a prior probability distribution over the unknown parameters or hypotheses. The prior represents our initial beliefs or knowledge about the parameters before observing the data. This can be based on expert knowledge, historical data, or other sources of information. In some cases, if we have little or no prior information, we may choose a non-informative prior, which assigns equal probability to all possible values of the parameter.
- **Likelihood**: The likelihood function represents the probability of observing the data given a specific value of the unknown parameter or hypothesis. It quantifies how consistent the data is with different parameter values. In Bayesian inference, we evaluate the likelihood of the data under different parameter values to determine how well each value explains the observed data.
- **Posterior probability**: Using Bayes' theorem, we combine the prior probability and the likelihood to obtain the posterior probability distribution. The posterior distribution

represents our updated beliefs about the unknown parameter or hypothesis after taking into account the observed data. The posterior distribution is the main result of Bayesian inference, and it allows us to make probabilistic statements about the unknown quantities.

- **Prediction and decision-making**: Once we have the posterior distribution, we can use it to make predictions about future data or make decisions based on our updated beliefs. This can involve computing point estimates (e.g., the mean or median of the posterior distribution), credible intervals (intervals containing a specified probability mass of the posterior distribution), or other quantities of interest. We can also use the posterior distribution to perform model comparison or selection, as discussed in the previous section.

Bayesian inference has several advantages over classical frequentist inference, such as the ability to incorporate prior knowledge, handle uncertainty in a natural way, and update our beliefs in a sequential manner. However, it also comes with some challenges, such as the choice of prior distributions and the computational complexity of evaluating the posterior distribution, especially for high-dimensional or complex models.

Bayesian Inference Procedure

To carry out Bayesian inference in Rust, follow these six steps, which encompass the preparation, execution, and interpretation of the process:

- Load and filter the dataset: Begin by loading your dataset into Rust and filtering it to retain only the data points that are relevant to your analysis. This initial step is crucial for ensuring that the subsequent steps are performed on accurate and representative data.
- Choose a prior distribution: Based on your existing knowledge or beliefs, select an appropriate prior distribution for the unknown parameter(s) of interest. This distribution represents your initial assumptions about the parameters before incorporating the evidence from the data.
- Define a likelihood function: Create a likelihood function that signifies the probability of observing the data given the unknown parameter(s). This function plays a critical role in connecting your data with your prior beliefs, allowing for the updating of your beliefs based on the evidence at hand.
- Use an MCMC method: Implement a Markov Chain Monte Carlo (MCMC) technique, such as the Metropolis-Hastings algorithm, to generate samples from the posterior distribution. This process enables the exploration of the parameter space and the estimation of the distribution that combines your prior beliefs with the data evidence.
- Compute relevant statistics: With the posterior samples obtained from the MCMC method, compute pertinent statistics such as the posterior mean, mode, and credible intervals. These statistics offer a comprehensive understanding of the parameter estimates and the uncertainty surrounding them.

- Interpret the results: Finally, analyze and interpret the computed statistics to draw meaningful conclusions about the unknown parameter(s) based on the Bayesian inference. This step may involve comparing different models, assessing the impact of your prior beliefs, or making predictions for future data points.

By adhering to these steps, you can effectively apply Bayesian inference in Rust to update your beliefs, quantify uncertainty, and make informed decisions based on the combination of prior knowledge and observed data.

Putting Bayesian Inference into Action

Let's estimate the average salary (μ) of Data Scientists using Bayesian inference. Here:

- We will use a prior belief about the average salary.
- We must update this belief based on the observed salaries from the dataset. The posterior distribution of the average salary is computed.
- You will then interpret the results, including the posterior mean and credible intervals.

So first, let's load the dataset and filter it for Data Scientists:

```
use csv::ReaderBuilder;
use ndarray::Array1;
use std::error::Error;
fn load_data() -> Result<Array1<f64>, Box<dyn Error>> {
    let mut rdr = ReaderBuilder::new()
        .has_headers(true)
        .from_path("ds_salaries.csv")?;
    let mut salaries = Vec::new();
    for result in rdr.records() {
        let record = result?;
        let job_title = record.get(3).unwrap();
        if job_title == "Data Scientist" {
            let salary: f64 = record.get(4).unwrap().parse()?;
            salaries.push(salary);
        }
```

```
    }
    Ok(Array1::from(salaries))
}
```

Now, we need to choose a prior distribution for the average salary. Since we're dealing with a continuous positive-valued variable (salary), a common choice for the prior distribution is the log-normal distribution.

So, lets assume that the average salary of Data Scientists follows a Normal distribution.

Let's use a prior $\mu \sim N(\mu_0, \sigma_2^0)$, where:

- μ_0=100,000: Our initial belief about the average salary.
- σ_0=20,000: Our uncertainty about this estimate.

Next, define the likelihood function. assuming the observed salaries are normally distributed around the true average salary μ\muμ with known variance σ2\sigma^2σ2:

$$P(D|\mu) = \prod_{i=1}^{n} \frac{1}{\sqrt{2\pi}\sigma} \exp\left(-\frac{(x_i - \mu)^2}{2\sigma^2}\right)$$

We can also use the sample standard deviation as an estimate for σ\sigmaσ.

Next, we then implement the Metropolis-Hastings Algorithm.

```
use rand::prelude::*;
use statrs::distribution::{Normal, Continuous};
fn metropolis_hastings(
    data: &Array1<f64>,
    prior_mean: f64,
    prior_std: f64,
    likelihood_std: f64,
    initial_mu: f64,
    iterations: usize,
) -> Vec<f64> {
    let mut rng = thread_rng();
    let mut mu_current = initial_mu;
```

```
    let mut samples = Vec::new();
    let prior = Normal::new(prior_mean, prior_std).unwrap();
    let likelihood = |mu: f64| {
        data.iter()
            .map(|&x| Normal::new(mu,
likelihood_std).unwrap().pdf(x))
            .product::<f64>()
    };
    for _ in 0..iterations {
        let mu_proposal = Normal::new(mu_current,
5000.0).unwrap().sample(&mut rng);
        let acceptance_ratio = (likelihood(mu_proposal) *
prior.pdf(mu_proposal))
            / (likelihood(mu_current) *
prior.pdf(mu_current));
        if acceptance_ratio >= 1.0 || rng.gen::<f64>() <
acceptance_ratio {
            mu_current = mu_proposal;
        }
        samples.push(mu_current);
    }
    samples
}
```

Now, generate posterior samples:

```
fn main() -> Result<(), Box<dyn Error>> {
    let data = load_data()?;
    let prior_mean = 100_000.0;
    let prior_std = 20_000.0;
    let likelihood_std = data.std(0.0);
    let initial_mu = data.mean().unwrap();
```

```
    let iterations = 10_000;
    let samples = metropolis_hastings(
        &data,
        prior_mean,
        prior_std,
        likelihood_std,
        initial_mu,
        iterations,
    );
    // Discard burn-in period
    let burn_in = 1000;
    let posterior_samples = &samples[burn_in..];
    // Compute statistics
    let posterior_mean = posterior_samples.iter().sum::<f64>()
/ posterior_samples.len() as f64;
    let posterior_std = (posterior_samples
        .iter()
        .map(|&x| (x - posterior_mean).powi(2))
        .sum::<f64>()
        / posterior_samples.len() as f64)
        .sqrt();
    println!("Posterior Mean: {:.2}", posterior_mean);
    println!("Posterior Std Dev: {:.2}", posterior_std);
    // Compute 95% credible interval
    let mut sorted_samples = posterior_samples.to_vec();
    sorted_samples.sort_by(|a, b| a.partial_cmp(b).unwrap());
    let lower_idx = (0.025 * sorted_samples.len() as
f64).floor() as usize;
    let upper_idx = (0.975 * sorted_samples.len() as
f64).floor() as usize;
```

```
    let credible_interval = (
        sorted_samples[lower_idx],
        sorted_samples[upper_idx],
    );
    println!(
        "95% Credible Interval: ({:.2}, {:.2})",
        credible_interval.0, credible_interval.1
    );
    Ok(())
}
```

Interpret the Results considering the output is:

```
Posterior Mean: 105,000.00
Posterior Std Dev: 5,000.00
95% Credible Interval: (95,000.00, 115,000.00)
```

The correct interpretation is as follows:

- Our updated belief about the average salary of data scientists is $105,000. This figure is the result of combining prior knowledge with observed data.
- This Posterior Standard Deviation estimate is uncertain to the extent of $5,000.
- And, we are 95% confident that the true average salary lies between $95,000 and $115,000.

This shows how Bayesian inference lets us update our beliefs based on new data, giving us a probabilistic understanding of the parameter estimates.

Advanced Markov Chain Monte Carlo Methods

Introduction to Hamiltonian Monte Carlo (HMC)

Hamiltonian Monte Carlo (HMC) is an advanced Markov Chain Monte Carlo (MCMC) method that generates samples from a target distribution more efficiently compared to other methods like the Metropolis-Hastings algorithm or Gibbs sampling. HMC leverages the concepts of Hamiltonian mechanics and gradient information of the target distribution to propose samples that are less correlated and lead to faster convergence.

HMC simulates a physical system where a particle moves through the parameter space under the influence of a potential energy field and a kinetic energy term. The potential energy corresponds to the negative log probability of the target distribution, while the kinetic energy is associated with a momentum variable introduced for each parameter in the model. The method then alternates between sampling the momentum variables from a Gaussian distribution and simulating the particle's motion through the parameter space using Hamilton's equations, which are a set of differential equations that describe the system's dynamics. The advantage of HMC over other MCMC methods is that it can more effectively explore high-dimensional or complex distributions, as it uses gradient information to guide the exploration and avoids random walk behavior. This can lead to faster convergence, fewer correlated samples, and more accurate estimates of the posterior distribution.

Following are the benefits of HMC:

- **Efficiency**: Produces less correlated samples, requiring fewer iterations to explore the posterior.
- **Scalability**: Handles high-dimensional problems more effectively.
- **Adaptivity**: Can adjust step sizes and trajectories to navigate complex posteriors.

Implementing HMC

Implementing HMC requires:

Computing the **gradient** of the log-posterior with respect to the parameters.

Implementing the **leapfrog integrator** to simulate Hamiltonian dynamics.

Ensuring **numerical stability** and accuracy.

While a full implementation is beyond the scope of this chapter, we can outline the steps.

- Load and preprocess the dataset as described in previous section.
- Choose a prior distribution and define the likelihood function for your model.
- Implement the Hamiltonian Monte Carlo algorithm, which involves:
    - Defining a function to compute the gradient of the log posterior distribution (negative potential energy) with respect to the parameters.
    - Implementing the leapfrog integration method, which approximates the solution to Hamilton's equations and simulates the particle's motion through the parameter space.
    - Proposing new samples based on the simulated particle's trajectory and accepting or rejecting them according to the Metropolis-Hastings acceptance criterion.
- Run the HMC algorithm to generate samples from the posterior distribution.

- Compute relevant statistics, such as the posterior mean and credible intervals, from the posterior samples.

The general idea of the above implementation is to leverage the gradient information to more efficiently explore the parameter space and generate samples from the posterior distribution. If you are interested in implementing HMC in Rust, you may want to refer to resources on the HMC algorithm and its implementation in other programming languages, such as Python or R, to gain more knowledge as these programming languages are heavily explored for statistics than Rust. For more advanced Bayesian modeling, consider using external tools or languages like **PyMC3** or **Stan** and interfacing them with Rust, or contributing to the development of Rust-based Bayesian libraries.

Model Comparison and Selection

Importance of Model Comparison

Model comparison and selection play a pivotal role in data analysis, as they facilitate the identification of the most appropriate model for a given problem. Within the Bayesian framework, several methods can be employed to compare models, including the Bayes factor, the Deviance Information Criterion (DIC), and the widely applicable information criterion (WAIC).

- The Bayes factor compares the marginal likelihoods of two competing models, M1 and M2. The marginal likelihood is the probability of the observed data under each model, after integrating out the unknown parameters. A larger Bayes factor indicates stronger evidence in favor of one model over the other. The Bayes factor can be difficult to compute, especially for complex models, as it requires integration over the parameter space.

- The DIC is a model selection criterion that balances model fit with model complexity. It is based on the deviance, a measure of model fit, and includes a penalty term for the number of effective parameters in the model. Lower DIC values indicate better models. The DIC can be easily computed from the posterior samples generated by MCMC methods, making it a convenient choice for model comparison.

- Similarly, the widely applicable information criterion (WAIC) estimates the predictive accuracy of a model while considering model complexity. Like DIC, lower WAIC values are preferable, as they signify a better trade-off between fit and complexity.

These model comparison methods enable analysts to make informed decisions about which Bayesian model to select, striking the right balance between explanatory power and model complexity. This careful selection process ultimately leads to more accurate and reliable predictions and inferences.

Model Comparison using DIC

The given below is a sample demonstration of model comparison using the Deviance Information Criterion (DIC) on the given dataset:

Suppose we have two competing models for predicting the salary of data science professionals:

- Model 1: salary ~ experience_level + job_title
- Model 2: salary ~ experience_level + job_title + company_size

First, fit both models using Bayesian regression and generate posterior samples using an MCMC method like the Metropolis-Hastings algorithm, Gibbs sampling, or HMC. For this demonstration, I'll assume you have already generated the posterior samples.

Next, compute DIC for Each Model:

```
fn compute_dic(log_likelihoods: &Array1<f64>,
effective_parameters: f64) -> f64
{
    let mean_deviance = -2.0 *
log_likelihoods.mean().unwrap();
    let dic = mean_deviance + 2.0 * effective_parameters;
    dic
}
```

Compare the DIC values of the two models. The model with the lower DIC is preferred, as it balances model fit and complexity better. In the above program, if dic_model_1 is lower than dic_model_2, then Model 1 is considered the better model; otherwise, Model 2 is preferred.

Model Comparison using WAIC

Let's perform model comparison using the Widely Applicable Information Criterion (WAIC) on the given dataset. Continuing from the previous example of DIC, we have two competing models for predicting the salary of data science professionals:

- Model 1: salary ~ experience_level + job_title
- Model 2: salary ~ experience_level + job_title + company_size

First, fit both models using Bayesian regression and generate posterior samples using an MCMC method like the Metropolis-Hastings algorithm, Gibbs sampling, or HMC. For this demonstration, I'll assume you have already generated the posterior samples.

Next, compute the WAIC for each model:

```
fn compute_lppd(log_likelihoods: &Array2<f64>) -> f64
{
    log_likelihoods
        .axis_iter(Axis(0))
        .map(|ll| {
            let max_ll = ll.fold(f64::NEG_INFINITY, |a, &b|
a.max(b));
            let sum_exp = ll.mapv(|x| (x -
max_ll).exp()).sum();
            max_ll + sum_exp.ln()
        })
        .sum()
}
fn compute_waic(log_likelihoods: &Array2<f64>) -> f64
{
    let lppd = compute_lppd(log_likelihoods);
    let p_waic = 2.0 * (lppd -
log_likelihoods.mean_axis(Axis(1)).unwrap().sum());
    -2.0 * lppd + 2.0 * p_waic
}
```

Compare the WAIC values of the two models. The model with the lower WAIC is preferred, as it balances model fit and complexity better. In the above sample program, if waic_model_1 is lower than waic_model_2, then Model 1 is considered the better model; otherwise, Model 2 is preferred.

Summary

In conclusion, this chapter has provided you with a good foundational understanding of machine learning. Through the utilization of Rust's libraries, you were able to implement supervised learning algorithms such as KNN as well as unsupervised methods such as k-means clustering. You were able to gain an understanding of the operation of these algorithms as well as their practical applications thanks to this hands-on experience.

In addition to that, you gained knowledge regarding the methods of model evaluation, such as cross-validation and performance metrics. You have improved your ability to evaluate and enhance models by applying these methods, which increases the likelihood that they will generalize well to new data. The subsequent chapters will cover more advanced machine learning topics and applications, and these foundational skills will prepare you for those topics and applications.

CHAPTER 8: MULTIVARIATE STATISTICAL METHODS

Introduction

This chapter digs into multivariate statistical methods, with a particular emphasis on techniques that deal with multiple variables at the same time. The Principal Component Analysis (PCA), the Canonical Correlation Analysis (CCA), and the Linear Discriminant Analysis (LDA) will all be something that you look into. These techniques will be implemented by you in order to reduce the dimensionality of complex datasets and to recognize patterns within them.

Throughout this chapter, the mathematical foundations of these techniques are emphasized, which will assist you in understanding when and how to apply a particular technique. In addition to gaining an understanding of data structure, you will acquire the ability to interpret results, such as principal components and discriminant functions. You will be able to improve your ability to analyze high-dimensional data by studying and becoming proficient in multivariate methods.

Principal Component Analysis (PCA)

Multivariate statistical methods involve the analysis of data with multiple variables, which allows us to understand the relationships and interactions among these variables. As opposed to univariate or bivariate methods, which focus on single or pairs of variables, multivariate techniques can provide a more comprehensive view of complex datasets. This can lead to better decision-making, improved predictions, and deeper insights into the underlying structures of the data. Multivariate statistical methods have gained significance in various fields, such as economics, biology, social sciences, and engineering, due to their ability to handle high-dimensional data and uncover hidden patterns.

Here, we will discuss some key multivariate techniques, their importance, and the breakthroughs they bring to statistical challenges. We begin with PCA as follows:

Understanding PCA

PCA is a prevalent multivariate method employed for dimensionality reduction in various fields, including machine learning, data analysis, and visualization. The primary objective of PCA is to generate a new set of uncorrelated variables, referred to as principal components. These components encapsulate most of the variance present in the original dataset while simultaneously reducing the overall number of dimensions, which helps mitigate the curse of dimensionality and facilitate more efficient analysis.

The mathematical underpinnings of PCA are rooted in linear algebra and eigenvalue decomposition. PCA starts by calculating the covariance matrix of the dataset, which quantifies the degree of correlation between the different features. Subsequently, it performs eigenvalue decomposition on this matrix to identify its eigenvectors and eigenvalues. These eigenvectors represent the principal components of the data, while their corresponding eigenvalues indicate the amount of variance captured by each component. The components are then sorted in descending order based on their eigenvalues, ensuring that the first principal component accounts for the largest proportion of variance, the second component captures the next largest proportion, and so on. By selecting a subset of principal components, we can effectively reduce the dimensionality of the dataset while preserving most of its inherent structure and information.

Procedure of PCA

Following is a step-by-step walkthrough to the mathematical architecture of PCA:

- **Standardize the dataset**: Since PCA is sensitive to the scale of the variables, it's essential to standardize the dataset, so each variable has a mean of 0 and a standard deviation of 1.
- **Calculate covariance matrix**: This step involves calculating the covariance matrix of the standardized dataset. The covariance matrix quantifies the linear relationship between each pair of variables in the dataset.
- **Compute eigenvalues and eigenvectors of covariance matrix**: Eigenvalues and eigenvectors are crucial in determining the principal components. Eigenvectors represent the direction of the principal components, while eigenvalues represent the magnitude of the variance captured by each component.
- **Sort eigenvalues and select top k eigenvectors**: The number of selected eigenvectors (k) determines the number of principal components retained in the analysis. These eigenvectors form a matrix called the loading matrix.
- **Project original dataset onto loading matrix**: Multiply the standardized dataset by the loading matrix to obtain the new set of principal components.

Now, let's implement the above procedure in the next topic.

Implementing PCA

Here, we will use the **ndarray** and **ndarray-linalg** crates for numerical computations.

At first, load and standardize the data:

```
use ndarray::Array2;
use ndarray::prelude::*;
use ndarray_stats::QuantileExt;
use std::error::Error;
// Function to standardize data
fn standardize_data(data: &Array2<f64>) -> Array2<f64> {
    let mean = data.mean_axis(Axis(0)).unwrap();
    let std_dev = data.std_axis(Axis(0), 0.0);
```

```
    (data - &mean) / &std_dev
}
```

-Next, compute the covariance matrix:

```
fn compute_covariance_matrix(data: &Array2<f64>) ->
Array2<f64> {
    let n_samples = data.nrows() as f64;
    data.t().dot(data) / (n_samples - 1.0)
}
```

Then, perform eigenvalue decomposition:

```
use ndarray_linalg::Eigen;

fn eigen_decomposition(cov_matrix: &Array2<f64>) ->
Result<(Array1<f64>, Array2<f64>), Box<dyn Error>> {
    let (eigenvalues, eigenvectors) = cov_matrix.eig()?;
    Ok((eigenvalues.re, eigenvectors.re))
}
```

Next, is to select principal components:

```
fn select_top_k_components(eigenvalues: &Array1<f64>,
eigenvectors: &Array2<f64>, k: usize) -> Array2<f64> {
    let mut eig_pairs: Vec<(f64, Array1<f64>)> = eigenvalues
        .iter()
        .zip(eigenvectors.axis_iter(Axis(1)))
        .map(|(&val, vec)| (val, vec.to_owned()))
        .collect();
    // Sort eigenvalues in descending order
    eig_pairs.sort_by(|a, b| b.0.partial_cmp(&a.0).unwrap());
    // Select top k eigenvectors
    let components = eig_pairs
        .iter()
```

```
        .take(k)
        .map(|(_, vec)| vec.clone())
        .collect::<Vec<Array1<f64>>>();
    // Stack selected eigenvectors horizontally
    let principal_components = Array2::from_shape_vec(
        (components[0].len(), k),
        components.into_iter().flat_map(|x|
x.to_vec()).collect(),
    )
    .unwrap();
    principal_components
}
```

Then transform the data:

```
fn transform_data(data: &Array2<f64>, components:
&Array2<f64>) -> Array2<f64> {
    data.dot(components)
}
```

In the result, the sum of the selected eigenvalues divided by the total sum of eigenvalues indicates how much variance is captured. In PCA, the eigenvectors represent the weights of the original variables in each principal component.

Canonical Correlation Analysis (CCA)

Understanding CCA

Canonical Correlation Analysis (CCA) is a sophisticated statistical technique employed to investigate the associations between two sets of multivariate variables. Its primary objective is to identify linear combinations of variables from both sets that exhibit the highest degree of correlation. In doing so, CCA helps uncover underlying patterns and relationships between the variables, which can then be utilized for further analysis or interpretation. CCA operates by computing the canonical variates, which are linear combinations of variables from each set. The coefficients of these linear combinations, known as canonical weights, are chosen to maximize the correlation between the canonical variates. Through this process, CCA yields multiple pairs of canonical variates and their corresponding canonical correlations, which indicate the strength of the relationships between the variables.

This technique is particularly useful in situations where researchers aim to explore the complex relationships between two multivariate data sets, such as psychological, socioeconomic, or environmental factors. Additionally, CCA can be applied to reduce the dimensionality of the data, making it more manageable and easier to analyze. However, it is important to note that CCA assumes linearity in the relationships between variables and requires a large sample size to ensure the stability of the estimated correlations. Furthermore, the interpretation of the canonical variates can sometimes be challenging, as they may not have a direct or clear meaning in the context of the original data. Despite these limitations, CCA remains a valuable technique for researchers seeking to uncover meaningful connections between two sets of multivariate variables.

Putting CCA into Action

Below is a quick implementation overview of the CCA algorithm:

- **Standardize the datasets**: Similar to PCA, CCA also requires the data to be standardized, with each variable having a mean of 0 and a standard deviation of 1.
- **Calculate the cross-covariance matrix**: Compute the cross-covariance matrix between the two sets of variables. This matrix captures the relationships between the variables in both sets.
- **Compute eigenvalues and eigenvectors of cross-covariance matrix**: Similar to PCA, the eigenvalues and eigenvectors are essential for determining the canonical correlations and weights.
- **Sort eigenvalues and select top k eigenvectors**: These eigenvectors form the canonical weights for each set of variables.
- **Calculate canonical correlations and canonical variates**: Here, use the canonical weights to compute the canonical correlations (the correlation between the canonical variates) and the canonical variates (the linear combinations of variables).

Now, let's implement CCA in the following:

First, standardize the data and compute covariance matrices:

```
fn standardize(data: &Array2<f64>) -> Array2<f64> {
    let mean = data.mean_axis(Axis(0)).unwrap();
    let std_dev = data.std_axis(Axis(0), 0.0);
    (data - &mean) / &std_dev
}
```

```
fn compute_covariance_matrices(
    x: &Array2<f64>,
    y: &Array2<f64>,
) -> (Array2<f64>, Array2<f64>, Array2<f64>) {
    let n_samples = x.nrows() as f64;
    let c_xx = x.t().dot(x) / (n_samples - 1.0);
    let c_yy = y.t().dot(y) / (n_samples - 1.0);
    let c_xy = x.t().dot(y) / (n_samples - 1.0);
    (c_xx, c_yy, c_xy)
}
```

Then, solve the generalized eigenvalue problem:

$$C_{XX}^{-1} C_{XY} C_{YY}^{-1} C_{YX} a = \rho^2 a$$

This can be computationally intensive, but we can simplify using Singular Value Decomposition (SVD) as shown below:

```
use ndarray_linalg::SVD;
fn perform_cca(x: &Array2<f64>, y: &Array2<f64>) ->
Result<(Array2<f64>, Array2<f64>), Box<dyn Error>> {
    // Standardize the data
    let x_std = standardize(x);
    let y_std = standardize(y);
    // Compute covariance matrices
    let (c_xx, c_yy, c_xy) =
compute_covariance_matrices(&x_std, &y_std);
    // Perform SVD on the covariance matrices
    let svd_x = c_xx.svd(true, true)?;
    let svd_y = c_yy.svd(true, true)?;
    // Whiten the data
    let k_x = svd_x.s.unwrap().mapv(|x| x.sqrt().recip());
```

```
    let k_y = svd_y.s.unwrap().mapv(|x| x.sqrt().recip());
    let white_x =
svd_x.u.unwrap().dot(&Array2::from_diag(&k_x));
    let white_y =
svd_y.u.unwrap().dot(&Array2::from_diag(&k_y));
    // Compute cross-covariance in whitened space
    let t = white_x.t().dot(&c_xy).dot(&white_y);
    // SVD of the whitened cross-covariance
    let svd_t = t.svd(true, true)?;
    let a = white_x.dot(&svd_t.u.unwrap());
    let b = white_y.dot(&svd_t.v_t.unwrap().t());
    Ok((a, b))
}
```

Here, the singular values from the SVD of t are the canonical correlations.

```
fn compute_canonical_correlations(singular_values:
&Array1<f64>) -> Array1<f64> {
    singular_values.clone()
}
```

Now, to arrive at the result, we can measure the strength of the association between the canonical variates. We can also identify the linear combinations of the original variables that are maximally correlated.

Linear Discriminant Analysis (LDA)

Understanding LDA

Linear Discriminant Analysis (LDA) is a widely-used technique in the realms of classification and dimensionality reduction. Its primary goal is to identify the most effective linear combinations of features that can optimally distinguish between two or more classes. This is accomplished by maximizing the distance between class means and minimizing the within-class scatter. LDA operates under the assumption that the data is normally distributed and that the classes share identical covariance matrices. These assumptions help simplify the computation process and provide a linear boundary for separating the classes.

Despite its linear nature, LDA can be remarkably effective in various scenarios. It excels in cases where the data adheres to the underlying assumptions, leading to improved classification performance. Additionally, the dimensionality reduction aspect of LDA can assist in mitigating the curse of dimensionality and reduce the risk of overfitting, ultimately enhancing the model's generalization capabilities. However, LDA's reliance on these assumptions can also be a limitation when dealing with data that does not follow a normal distribution or exhibits dissimilar covariance matrices across classes. In such cases, alternative methods, such as Quadratic Discriminant Analysis (QDA) or non-linear classifiers, might be more suitable.

Performing LDA Algorithm

Below is an overview of the LDA algorithm:

- Compute the mean of each class: Calculate the mean vector for each class.
- Calculate the within-class scatter matrix: Compute the scatter matrix for each class and then sum them up to obtain the within-class scatter matrix.
- Calculate the between-class scatter matrix: Compute the scatter matrix between the classes.
- Compute the eigenvalues and eigenvectors of the matrix product of the inverse of the within-class scatter matrix and the between-class scatter matrix.
- Sort the eigenvalues in descending order and select the top k eigenvectors corresponding to the k largest eigenvalues: These eigenvectors form the LDA transformation matrix.
- Apply the LDA transformation matrix to the original dataset to obtain the transformed dataset.

Now, let's implement LDA on the given dataset using the ndarray considering that we have class labels.

```
use ndarray::Array1;

struct Dataset {

    data: Array2<f64>,

    labels: Array1<usize>,

}
```

We then compute class means:

```
use std::collections::HashMap;

fn compute_class_means(dataset: &Dataset) -> HashMap<usize,
Array1<f64>> {
```

```
    let mut class_sums = HashMap::new();
    let mut class_counts = HashMap::new();
    for (i, row) in
dataset.data.axis_iter(Axis(0)).enumerate() {
        let label = dataset.labels[i];
        class_sums
            .entry(label)
            .and_modify(|sum| *sum += &row)
            .or_insert_with(|| row.to_owned());
        *class_counts.entry(label).or_insert(0) += 1;
    }
    class_sums
        .into_iter()
        .map(|(label, sum)| {
            let count = class_counts[&label] as f64;
            (label, sum / count)
        })
        .collect()
}
```

Next, we compute scatter matrices:

```
fn compute_scatter_matrices(
    dataset: &Dataset,
    class_means: &HashMap<usize, Array1<f64>>,
) -> (Array2<f64>, Array2<f64>) {
    let n_features = dataset.data.ncols();
    let mut s_w = Array2::<f64>::zeros((n_features,
n_features));
    let mut s_b = Array2::<f64>::zeros((n_features,
n_features));
```

```
    let overall_mean =
dataset.data.mean_axis(Axis(0)).unwrap();
    for (&label, class_mean) in class_means {
        let class_data = dataset
            .data
            .outer_iter()
            .zip(dataset.labels.iter())
            .filter(|&(_, &l)| l == label)
            .map(|(x, _)| x.to_owned())
            .collect::<Vec<_>>();
        let class_scatter = class_data.iter().fold(
            Array2::<f64>::zeros((n_features, n_features)),
            |acc, x| {
                let diff = x - class_mean;
                acc +
diff.view().to_owned().insert_axis(Axis(1)).dot(

&diff.view().to_owned().insert_axis(Axis(0)),
                )
            },
        );
        s_w += &class_scatter;
        let n_i = class_data.len() as f64;
        let mean_diff = class_mean - &overall_mean;
        s_b += n_i *
mean_diff.view().insert_axis(Axis(1)).dot(&mean_diff.view().in
sert_axis(Axis(0)));
    }
    (s_w, s_b)
}
```

Then, we solve the generalized eigenvalue problem:

```
fn solve_eigen_problem(s_w: &Array2<f64>, s_b: &Array2<f64>) -
> Result<Array2<f64>, Box<dyn Error>> {
    let s_w_inv = s_w.inv()?;
    let matrix = s_w_inv.dot(s_b);
    let (eigenvalues, eigenvectors) = matrix.eig()?;
    // Sort eigenvectors by eigenvalues
    let mut eig_pairs: Vec<(f64, Array1<f64>)> = eigenvalues
        .re
        .iter()
        .zip(eigenvectors.re.axis_iter(Axis(1)))
        .map(|(&val, vec)| (val, vec.to_owned()))
        .collect();
    eig_pairs.sort_by(|a, b| b.0.partial_cmp(&a.0).unwrap());
    // Stack eigenvectors horizontally
    let w = Array2::from_shape_vec(
        (eig_pairs[0].1.len(), eig_pairs.len()),
        eig_pairs.into_iter().flat_map(|(_, vec)|
vec.to_vec()).collect(),
    )?;
    Ok(w)
}
```

Next, we transform the data:

```
fn transform_data(data: &Array2<f64>, w: &Array2<f64>, k:
usize) -> Array2<f64> {
    let w_reduced = w.slice(s![.., 0..k]);
    data.dot(&w_reduced)
}
```

The results are clear. The transformed data speaks for itself. The data has been projected onto a lower-dimensional space that maximizes class separability.

Independent Component Analysis (ICA)

Understanding ICA

Independent Component Analysis (ICA) is a prominent multivariate statistical technique primarily employed for blind source separation or feature extraction. The central aim of ICA is to disentangle a set of mixed signals into their original sources, with the assumption that these sources are non-Gaussian and statistically independent from one another. ICA's underlying principle is based on the idea that the observed data is a linear mixture of independent components. The technique strives to recover the original sources by estimating a demixing matrix, which, when applied to the observed data, yields the independent components.

One key distinction between ICA and other methods such as Principal Component Analysis (PCA) lies in their objectives. PCA concentrates on minimizing the variance and discovering orthogonal components, whereas ICA focuses on identifying statistically independent components. This difference in focus makes ICA particularly useful for applications where the sources of interest exhibit statistical independence. ICA has found widespread adoption in diverse fields, such as image processing, where it can be employed to remove noise or artifacts; audio processing, where it can separate mixed audio signals into distinct sources, such as individual speakers or instruments; and financial data analysis, where it helps unveil hidden patterns in financial time series data or detect fraudulent activities.

Moreover, ICA has proven valuable in the field of neuroscience, particularly for analyzing electroencephalogram (EEG) and functional magnetic resonance imaging (fMRI) data, as it helps isolate distinct neural sources from the complex, mixed signals produced by the brain's electrical activity. Despite its many advantages, ICA does have some limitations, including its sensitivity to the initialization of the demixing matrix and its dependence on the assumption of non-Gaussian sources. Nevertheless, when applied appropriately, ICA serves as a powerful technique for uncovering hidden patterns and sources in various types of data.

Applying ICA

Now, let's implement ICA using the ndarray and ndarray-rand crates along with the FastICA algorithm:

First, center and whiten the data:

```
fn center_data(data: &Array2<f64>) -> Array2<f64> {
    let mean = data.mean_axis(Axis(0)).unwrap();
    data - &mean
```

```
}
fn whiten_data(data: &Array2<f64>) -> Result<Array2<f64>,
Box<dyn Error>> {
    let cov = compute_covariance_matrix(data);
    let (eigenvalues, eigenvectors) = cov.eig()?;
    let d = Array2::from_diag(
        &eigenvalues
            .re
            .mapv(|x| if x > 0.0 { x.recip().sqrt() } else {
0.0 }),
    );
    let whitening_matrix =
eigenvectors.re.dot(&d).dot(&eigenvectors.re.t());
    Ok(data.dot(&whitening_matrix))
}
```

Next, apply the FastICA algorithm:

```
use rand::prelude::*;
fn fast_ica(
    data: &Array2<f64>,
    n_components: usize,
    max_iter: usize,
    tol: f64,
) -> Result<Array2<f64>, Box<dyn Error>> {
    let mut rng = thread_rng();
    let n_features = data.ncols();
    let mut w = Array2::<f64>::random((n_components,
n_features), rand::distributions::StandardNormal);
    for _ in 0..max_iter {
        let w_old = w.clone();
        // Symmetric decorrelation
```

```
        let w_wt = w.dot(&w.t());
        let w_wt_inv_sqrt = w_wt.inv()?.sqrt()?.inv()?;
        w = w_wt_inv_sqrt.dot(&w);
        // Compute the projections
        let gwx = data.dot(&w.t()).mapv(|x| x.tanh());
        let g_wx = 1.0 - gwx.mapv(|x| x.powi(2));
        // Update weights
        let w_new = (gwx.t().dot(data) / data.nrows() as f64)
- &w * &g_wx.mean_axis(Axis(0)).unwrap().insert_axis(Axis(1));
        w = w_new;
        // Check for convergence
        let lim = (&w * &w_old).sum_axis(Axis(1)).mapv(|x| 1.0
- x.abs()).sum();
        if lim < tol {
            break;
        }
    }
    Ok(w)
}
```

The results can be interpreted as follows:

- It can be confirmed that the estimated source signals are statistically independent.
- The mixing matrix can be estimated as follows: A=W^(−1)A = W^(−1).

Multidimensional Scaling (MDS)

Understanding MDS

Multidimensional Scaling (MDS) is a versatile multivariate statistical technique that aims to visualize the similarity or dissimilarity between objects in a high-dimensional space by projecting them onto a lower-dimensional space, typically 2D or 3D. This technique is applicable across various fields, such as psychology, marketing, and network analysis, offering valuable insights into complex data.

The primary goal of MDS is to maintain the pairwise distances between objects as accurately as possible when mapping them to a lower-dimensional space. Now, this technique can be categorized into two main types:

Classical MDS (also known as Principal Coordinates Analysis): This type of MDS assumes that the input data comes in the form of a distance matrix. It employs eigendecomposition of the matrix to compute the lower-dimensional representation. Classical MDS works best when the data has a linear structure, and the actual distances between objects are crucial to the analysis.

Non-metric MDS: In contrast to Classical MDS, Non-metric MDS focuses on preserving the rank order of the distances between objects rather than the actual distances. This method is more suitable for data with non-linear relationships and is less sensitive to measurement scale differences. Non-metric MDS uses iterative optimization techniques, such as the stress majorization algorithm or the Shepard-Kruskal algorithm, to find the best-fitting configuration.

MDS's ability to reduce dimensionality while preserving critical relationships between objects makes it an essential asset in various research areas. Some common applications include the study of consumer preferences in marketing research, social network analysis, the examination of similarities in psychological traits, and the comparison of biological species in ecology.

Implementing MDS

Let's implement Classical MDS, starting with first we compute distance matrix:

```
fn compute_distance_matrix(data: &Array2<f64>) -> Array2<f64>
{
    let n = data.nrows();
    let mut dist_matrix = Array2::<f64>::zeros((n, n));
    for i in 0..n {
        for j in i..n {
            let dist = (&data.row(i) - &data.row(j)).mapv(|x|
x.powi(2)).sum().sqrt();
            dist_matrix[[i, j]] = dist;
            dist_matrix[[j, i]] = dist;
        }
    }
    dist_matrix
}
```

Then we apply Classical MDS as shown below:

```
fn classical_mds(dist_matrix: &Array2<f64>, n_components:
usize) -> Result<Array2<f64>, Box<dyn Error>> {
    let n = dist_matrix.nrows();
    // Centering matrix
    let h = Array2::<f64>::eye(n) -
Array2::<f64>::from_elem((n, n), 1.0 / n as f64);
    // Apply double centering
    let b = -0.5 * h.dot(&dist_matrix.mapv(|x|
x.powi(2))).dot(&h);
    // Eigen decomposition
    let (eigenvalues, eigenvectors) = b.eig()?;
    // Select top components
    let idx = eigenvalues.re
        .iter()
        .enumerate()
        .filter(|&(_, &val)| val > 0.0)
        .map(|(i, _)| i)
        .take(n_components)
        .collect::<Vec<_>>();
    let l = Array2::from_diag(
        &Array1::from(idx.iter().map(|&i|
eigenvalues.re[i].sqrt()).collect::<Vec<_>>()),
    );
    let e = eigenvectors.re.select(Axis(1), &idx);
    // Coordinates
    let x = e.dot(&l);
    Ok(x)
}
```

The results can be interpreted as coordinates which are low-dimensional representation of the data preserving the distance relationships. And then, the next step is to create a visualization by plotting the coordinates to visualize clusters or patterns.

Summary

You are now an expert in multivariate statistical methods after reading this chapter. Through the use of PCA, CCA, and LDA, which you implemented, you were able to effectively reduce the dimensionality of complex datasets and extract meaningful patterns from them. You were able to acquire a deeper understanding of the mathematical principles that underlie these methods by participating in coding exercises.

You gained the ability to interpret the results of multivariate analyses, such as eigenvalues and canonical correlations, which provided you with valuable insights into the relationships between the data. You will be equipped to confidently tackle advanced analytical challenges if you possess these skills, which are essential for fields that deal with large datasets that are complex.

CHAPTER 9: NONLINEAR MODELS AND MACHINE LEARNING

Overview

This chapter will provide you with a pathway to nonlinear models as well as advanced machine learning techniques. You are going to learn about ensemble methods such as random forests, decision trees, support vector machines (SVM), and neural networks. Implementing these models will allow you to handle complex and nonlinear relationships in data. You will do this by utilizing Rust's smartcore, linfa, and tch crates.

Throughout this chapter, the emphasis is placed on the understanding and practical application of these algorithms. The training of models, the tuning of hyperparameters, and the evaluation of performance will all be covered. Your analytical capabilities will be significantly improved by the time you reach the conclusion of this chapter because you will be able to use Rust to apply powerful machine learning models to problems that occur in the real world.

Introduction to Nonlinear Models and Machine Learning

Why Nonlinear Models?

Nonlinear models addresses complex data patterns that cannot be accurately represented by linear relationships. These models provide superior flexibility and adaptability in tackling real-world problems, where the connections between variables are frequently complex and nonlinear. They have proven to be invaluable tools in diverse domains such as finance, healthcare, and natural language processing, among others.

Some popular nonlinear models include:

- **Decision Trees**: These models recursively divide the data into subsets based on input features, forming a tree-like structure. Decision trees can be utilized for both regression and classification tasks. They are straightforward, easy to interpret, and robust to outliers. Moreover, they can handle both continuous and categorical variables.
- **Support Vector Machines (SVM)**: SVM is a versatile algorithm employed for classification and regression tasks. It seeks to find the optimal separating hyperplane (in the case of classification) or the best fitting hyperplane (in the case of regression) by maximizing the margin between classes or minimizing the regression error, respectively. SVMs can tackle linear and nonlinear problems using kernel functions, which map the data into a higher-dimensional space, thereby enabling the discovery of nonlinear relationships.
- **Neural Networks**: These are biologically-inspired models composed of interconnected nodes (neurons) organized into layers. Neural networks can approximate any continuous

function and are highly effective in learning complex patterns in large datasets. Deep learning, a subfield of machine learning, emphasizes neural networks with numerous hidden layers, facilitating the identification of intricate features in data. Applications of neural networks include image recognition, natural language processing, and game playing.

- **Ensemble Methods**: Ensemble methods combine multiple models to enhance predictive performance. Techniques such as bagging (Bootstrap Aggregating), boosting, and stacking are employed to reduce overfitting, increase accuracy, and make the model more robust. Popular ensemble methods encompass Random Forests, Gradient Boosting Machines (GBM), and XGBoost. These methods often outperform single-model approaches and are widely used in various machine learning competitions.

Machine Learning Breakthroughs

The progression of statistics into machine learning (ML) has been transformative, with ML algorithms furnishing potent tools for resolving intricate problems. Some key breakthroughs encompass:

- **Handling Large Datasets**: ML algorithms can effectively process and learn from vast amounts of data, facilitating the discovery of sophisticated patterns and relationships that would be challenging to uncover using conventional statistical methods.
- **Feature Learning**: ML techniques such as deep learning can automatically learn and extract pertinent features from raw data, eliminating the necessity for manual feature engineering. This capability significantly reduces the time and effort required for data preprocessing and allows for more accurate modeling.
- **Robustness and Adaptability**: ML models can adapt to alterations in data distributions and are frequently more robust to noise and outliers compared to traditional statistical models. This makes them suitable for handling real-world data, which often exhibits such characteristics.
- **Model Complexity**: ML models can capture intricate, nonlinear relationships in data, permitting them to model complex phenomena with greater accuracy. This enables the development of models that can address a wide range of problems, from simple linear regression to highly complex deep learning tasks.
- **Generalization**: ML algorithms can generalize well to unseen data, rendering them appropriate for predictive modeling and decision-making across various domains. This property is particularly important in situations where models must adapt to new, previously unseen data.
- **Automation and Scalability**: ML algorithms can be effortlessly automated and scaled to handle extensive datasets, rendering them indispensable in data-driven industries. This

allows organizations to process and analyze large volumes of data quickly and efficiently, enabling data-driven decision-making and insights.

Nonlinear models have become essential tools for handling complex data patterns that cannot be accurately captured by linear relationships. They offer greater flexibility and adaptability in addressing real-world problems, where relationships between variables are often intricate and nonlinear. With the ongoing advancement. In further topics, we will examine and implement each of these models and will explore how the linear relationships are well correlated and captured.

Decision Trees

Understanding Decision Trees

A decision tree is a versatile, flowchart-like structure used in machine learning and data mining for making decisions or predictions based on a set of input features. This tree-like structure consists of three primary components: internal nodes, branches, and leaf nodes. Internal nodes represent the decision points based on the values of the input features. Branches, on the other hand, signify the possible outcomes or consequences of those decisions. Lastly, leaf nodes symbolize the final decision or prediction made by the tree.

The construction of decision trees involves a recursive algorithm that iteratively selects the most suitable feature to split the dataset at each internal node. This selection process is guided by a specific criterion, such as Gini impurity or Information Gain. These criteria help determine the homogeneity of the resulting subsets, with the ultimate goal of maximizing the purity or information content of the splits. Decision trees offer several advantages, including their ability to handle both numerical and categorical data, their ease of interpretation, and their inherent feature selection capability. However, they are also prone to overfitting, which can be mitigated through techniques like pruning or by using ensemble methods like Random Forests or Gradient Boosting Machines.

Key Characteristics

Interpretability

Decision trees are easy to interpret and visualize, making them valuable for understanding the decision-making process.

Handling Different Data Types

They can handle both numerical and categorical data.

Feature Selection

They perform implicit feature selection by choosing the most informative features for splitting.

Nonlinear Boundaries

Capable of modeling complex decision boundaries by partitioning the feature space into rectangular regions.

Building a Decision Tree

The process of building a decision tree involves:

- Selecting the Best Feature to Split: Use criteria like **Gini Impurity**, **Entropy**, or **Information Gain** to measure the quality of a split.
- Recursive Partitioning: Split the dataset into subsets based on the selected feature.

Just repeat the process for each subset until you reach a stopping condition, such as reaching the maximum depth or having a minimum number of samples per leaf.

Implementing Decision Trees

We will implement a decision tree for regression. For this, we will aim to predict **salary_in_usd** based on various features.

To proceed, we will use the **smartcore** crate, which provides machine learning algorithms.

```
use smartcore::linalg::naive::dense_matrix::DenseMatrix;
use
smartcore::tree::decision_tree_regressor::{DecisionTreeRegress
or, DecisionTreeRegressorParameters};
use csv::ReaderBuilder;
use std::error::Error;
```

Next, split the dataset:

```
use rand::seq::SliceRandom;
use rand::thread_rng;
fn train_test_split(
    x: &DenseMatrix<f64>,
    y: &Vec<f64>,
    test_size: f64,
) -> (DenseMatrix<f64>, Vec<f64>, DenseMatrix<f64>, Vec<f64>)
{
```

```
    let mut indices: Vec<usize> = (0..y.len()).collect();
    indices.shuffle(&mut thread_rng());
    let test_size = (y.len() as f64 * test_size).round() as
usize;
    let test_indices = &indices[..test_size];
    let train_indices = &indices[test_size..];
    let x_train = x.select_rows(train_indices);
    let y_train = train_indices.iter().map(|&i|
y[i]).collect();
    let x_test = x.select_rows(test_indices);
    let y_test = test_indices.iter().map(|&i| y[i]).collect();
    (x_train, y_train, x_test, y_test)
}
```

Then, create and train the decision tree model:

```
fn main() -> Result<(), Box<dyn Error>> {
    let (x, y) = load_dataset()?;
    let (x_train, y_train, x_test, y_test) =
train_test_split(&x, &y, 0.2);
    let params = DecisionTreeRegressorParameters::default()
        .with_max_depth(Some(5))
        .with_min_samples_split(2);
    let tree = DecisionTreeRegressor::fit(&x_train, &y_train,
params)?;
    // Evaluate the model
    let y_pred = tree.predict(&x_test)?;
    let mse = mean_squared_error(&y_test, &y_pred);
    println!("Mean Squared Error: {}", mse);
    Ok(())
}
```

```
fn mean_squared_error(y_true: &Vec<f64>, y_pred: &Vec<f64>) ->
f64 {
    y_true
        .iter()
        .zip(y_pred.iter())
        .map(|(a, b)| (a - b).powi(2))
        .sum::<f64>()
        / y_true.len() as f64
}
```

Now, let's take a look at the results and see what they tell us. The first thing we'll look at is the Mean Squared Error, or MSE for short. It shows the average difference between what we predicted and what actually happened. The lower the value, the better the performance. And, the tree depth is the maximum depth of the tree controls how complex the model is. A deeper tree may overfit, while a shallower tree may underfit.

Support Vector Machines (SVM)

Understanding SVM

Next, we'll look at another well-known non-linear model: Support Vector Machines (SVM). SVMs are great at handling data that can be separated in either a linear or non-linear way. They do this by finding the best way to separate different groups of data using a line or boundary.

SVMs are based on the clever "kernel trick," which lets you project data into a higher-dimensional space. This transformation makes the data that couldn't be separated linearly now able to be separated, which means SVMs can find the best hyperplane. The kernel trick uses a whole range of kernel functions, like linear, polynomial, radial basis function (RBF), and sigmoid, to suit different data distributions and patterns. SVMs are great at generalizing and can handle a lot of different classification tasks. They're great at handling high-dimensional data and are less likely to overfit than some other machine learning models. However, they may need more computing power and careful tuning of the hyperparameters to get the best results. Thanks to these qualities, SVMs have become a go-to tool in machine learning.

Following are the types of Kernels:

- **Linear Kernel**: Used when data is linearly separable.
- **Polynomial Kernel**: Captures polynomial relationships.

- **Radial Basis Function (RBF) Kernel**: Also known as Gaussian kernel; suitable for nonlinear data.
- **Sigmoid Kernel**: Similar to a two-layer neural network.

Implementing SVM

We will use the **linfa** crate, which provides a pure Rust machine learning toolkit.

To begin with, first import required libraries:

```
use linfa::prelude::*;
use linfa_svm::Svm;
use linfa_svm::SvmParams;
use ndarray::Array2;
use ndarray::Array1;
use csv::ReaderBuilder;
use std::error::Error;
```

Next, we then load and preprocess the dataset, assuming we want to classify whether a job is remote or not based on other features.

```
fn load_dataset() -> Result<(Array2<f64>, Array1<u32>),
Box<dyn Error>> {
    let mut rdr = ReaderBuilder::new()
        .has_headers(true)
        .from_path("ds_salaries.csv")?;
    let mut features = Vec::new();
    let mut targets = Vec::new();
    for result in rdr.records() {
        let record = result?;
        let work_year: f64 = record.get(0).unwrap().parse()?;
        let experience_level = match record.get(1).unwrap() {
            "EN" => 0.0,
            "MI" => 1.0,
            "SE" => 2.0,
```

```
            "EX" => 3.0,
            _ => 0.0,
        };
        let remote_ratio: f64 =
record.get(8).unwrap().parse()?;
        let salary_in_usd: f64 =
record.get(4).unwrap().parse()?;
        features.push(vec![work_year, experience_level,
salary_in_usd]);
        // Binary target: 1 if remote_ratio > 0, else 0
        let is_remote = if remote_ratio > 0.0 { 1 } else { 0
};
        targets.push(is_remote);
    }
    let x = Array2::from(features);
    let y = Array1::from(targets);
    Ok((x, y))
}
```

Next, split the dataset:

```
use linfa::Dataset;
fn split_dataset(
    x: Array2<f64>,
    y: Array1<u32>,
) -> (Dataset<f64, u32>, Dataset<f64, u32>) {
    let dataset = Dataset::new(x, y);
    let (train, valid) =
dataset.shuffle(42).split_with_ratio(0.8);
    (train, valid)
}
```

Then, create and train the SVM model:

```
fn main() -> Result<(), Box<dyn Error>> {
    let (x, y) = load_dataset()?;
    let (train, valid) = split_dataset(x, y);
    // Create SVM with RBF kernel
    let params = SvmParams::default()
        .gaussian_kernel(50.0)
        .with_c(1.0);
    let model = params.fit(&train)?;
    // Evaluate the model
    let pred = model.predict(&valid);
    let cm = pred.confusion_matrix(&valid)?;
    println!("Accuracy: {:.2}%", cm.accuracy() * 100.0);
    Ok(())
}
```

How to read the results:

- **Accuracy**: This is the number of correct predictions we made.
- **Confusion Matrix**: It gives you the lowdown on true positives, true negatives, false positives, and false negatives.

Neural Networks

Understanding Neural Networks

Neural Networks represent a formidable category of machine learning models, especially adept at tackling intricate, high-dimensional data. Inspired by the human brain's neural structure, these networks consist of multiple layers of interconnected neurons, which are systematically organized into three primary groups: input, hidden, and output layers. The input layer is responsible for receiving raw data, while the output layer produces the final predictions or classifications. Between these two layers are the hidden layers, which perform complex transformations and feature extraction to enable the model to learn intricate patterns within the data. The neurons in each layer communicate through weighted connections, allowing information to flow from one layer to another.

One of the key strengths of Neural Networks is their ability to learn hierarchical representations, which means they can automatically identify and extract relevant features from the data without manual intervention. This makes them particularly effective in tasks such as image recognition, natural language processing, and speech recognition, where traditional algorithms struggle to cope with the complexity and scale of the data. Moreover, Neural Networks can be scaled up by adding more layers and neurons to increase their capacity for learning complex relationships, resulting in deep learning models known as Deep Neural Networks (DNNs). While their impressive capabilities come at the cost of increased computational demands and training time, the use of modern hardware accelerators like GPUs and dedicated AI chips has significantly improved their efficiency.

Following are the key components:

- **Input Layer**: Receives input features.
- **Hidden Layers**: Intermediate layers that perform computations and extract features.
- **Output Layer**: Produces the final prediction or classification.

The activation functions are:

- **Sigmoid**: Maps input to (0,1); used in binary classification.
- **ReLU**: **f(x) = max(0, x)**; helps with vanishing gradient problems.
- **Tanh**: Maps input to (-1,1); zero-centered.

Implementing Neural Networks

For building neural network, we will use the **tch** crate, which provides Rust bindings for PyTorch. To begin with, we first import required libraries and preprocess the dataset as shown below:

```
use tch::{nn, nn::ModuleT, nn::OptimizerConfig, Tensor, Kind,
Device};

use csv::ReaderBuilder;

use std::error::Error;

fn load_dataset() -> Result<(Tensor, Tensor), Box<dyn Error>>
{

    let mut rdr = ReaderBuilder::new()

        .has_headers(true)

        .from_path("ds_salaries.csv")?;

    let mut features = Vec::new();

    let mut targets = Vec::new();
```

```
    for result in rdr.records() {
        let record = result?;
        let work_year: f64 = record.get(0).unwrap().parse()?;
        let experience_level = match record.get(1).unwrap() {
            "EN" => 0.0,
            "MI" => 1.0,
            "SE" => 2.0,
            "EX" => 3.0,
            _ => 0.0,
        };
        let remote_ratio: f64 =
record.get(8).unwrap().parse()?;
        let salary_in_usd: f64 =
record.get(4).unwrap().parse()?;
        features.push([work_year, experience_level,
remote_ratio]);
        targets.push(salary_in_usd);
    }
    let x = Tensor::of_slice2(&features);
    let y = Tensor::of_slice(&targets).unsqueeze(1);
    Ok((x, y))
}
```

Next, define the neural network structure:

```
fn create_net(vs: &nn::Path) -> impl nn::ModuleT {
    nn::seq_t()
        .add(nn::linear(vs / "layer1", 3, 64,
Default::default()))
        .add_fn(|xs| xs.relu())
        .add(nn::linear(vs / "layer2", 64, 64,
Default::default()))
```

```
        .add_fn(|xs| xs.relu())
        .add(nn::linear(vs / "output", 64, 1,
Default::default()))
}
```

Then, train the neural network:

```
fn main() -> Result<(), Box<dyn Error>> {
    let (x, y) = load_dataset()?;
    let device = Device::cuda_if_available();
    let vs = nn::VarStore::new(device);
    let net = create_net(&vs.root());
    let mut opt = nn::Adam::default().build(&vs, 1e-3)?;
    let epochs = 1000;
    for epoch in 1..=epochs {
        let output = net
            .forward_t(&x.to_device(device), /* train */
true);
        let loss = output.mse_loss(&y.to_device(device),
tch::Reduction::Mean);
        opt.backward_step(&loss);
        if epoch % 100 == 0 {
            println!("Epoch: {}, Loss: {:?}", epoch,
f64::from(&loss));
        }
    }
    // Evaluate the model (you can split data into train/test
sets)
    Ok(())
}
```

Now interpret the results across:

- **Loss**: It's the Mean Squared Error between the predicted and actual values. Just keep an eye on the loss to make sure it gets smaller over time.
- **Overfitting**: If the loss on the training data goes down but the performance on the validation data goes down too, it could be that overfitting is happening.

Ensemble Methods

Understanding Ensemble Methods

Ensemble methods represent a category of machine learning techniques designed to improve accuracy and generalization by aggregating the predictions of multiple base models. This approach capitalizes on the strengths of individual models while mitigating their weaknesses, ultimately resulting in a more robust and accurate composite model.

There are several popular but very common ensemble techniques:

- **Bagging**, or **Bootstrap Aggregating**, is a technique where multiple base models are trained independently using random subsets of the training data, sampled with replacement. The final prediction is obtained by averaging the predictions (for regression tasks) or by taking a majority vote (for classification tasks) across all base models. Bagging helps reduce overfitting and variance while improving the overall stability of the model.
- **Boosting**, on the other hand, focuses on iteratively training base models to correct the errors of their predecessors. Each subsequent model places more emphasis on instances that were misclassified by the previous model. The final prediction is derived by weighting the predictions of all base models and then combining them. This method often leads to higher accuracy compared to bagging but may be more prone to overfitting.
- **Stacking**, also known as **Stacked Generalization**, is a technique that involves training multiple base models using different algorithms or configurations, and then training a higher-level meta-model to combine their predictions. The meta-model learns to optimally weigh and blend the predictions from the base models, leading to better overall performance.

These kinds of ensemble methods are used a lot in machine learning because they can make predictions more accurate, generalise better and be more robust.

Implementing Random Forests

We will implement a Random Forest, an ensemble of decision trees, using the **smartcore** crate. To begin with, let us use the same **load_dataset** and **train_test_split** function from the Decision Tree section.

Then, we create and train the random forest model

```
fn main() -> Result<(), Box<dyn Error>> {
    let (x, y) = load_dataset()?;
    let (x_train, y_train, x_test, y_test) =
train_test_split(&x, &y, 0.2);
    let params = RandomForestRegressorParameters::default()
        .with_n_estimators(100)
        .with_max_depth(Some(5))
        .with_min_samples_split(2);
    let rf = RandomForestRegressor::fit(&x_train, &y_train,
params)?;
    // Evaluate the model
    let y_pred = rf.predict(&x_test)?;
    let mse = mean_squared_error(&y_test, &y_pred);
    println!("Mean Squared Error: {}", mse);
    Ok(())
}
```

While you interpret the results, you will come across that Random Forests often outperform single decision trees by reducing overfitting.

Summary

In this chapter, we've explored the realm of **Nonlinear Models and Machine Learning**, focusing on their importance in handling complex data patterns that linear models cannot capture. Now that you have reached the conclusion of this chapter, you have added more sophisticated nonlinear models to your arsenal of machine learning technologies. You were able to implement decision trees, support vector machines (SVMs), neural networks, and ensemble methods, thereby gaining practical experience with sophisticated algorithms. There are complex data patterns that linear models are unable to capture, and you learned how to address them.

You also have a strong command of the techniques involved in model training, tuning of hyperparameters, and performance evaluation. Through the utilization of these methodologies, you have improved your capacity to construct robust models that are capable of generalization. These abilities are absolutely necessary in order to successfully complete complex machine learning tasks in a variety of different fields.

CHAPTER 10: MODEL EVALUATION AND VALIDATION

Introduction

The crucial procedures of model evaluation and validation are brought to the forefront in this chapter. You will learn how to evaluate model performance, avoid overfitting, and ensure generalizability to new data. The chapter teaches methods like train-test split, cross-validation, hyperparameter tuning, and model selection criteria like AIC and BIC. You will apply these evaluation techniques to machine learning models, increasing their reliability. You will understand the significance of metrics, confusion matrices, and resampling techniques such as bootstrapping. The robustness and credibility of your analytical results will be improved if you are able to master the process of model evaluation.

The Importance of Model Evaluation and Validation

Why Model Evaluation?

Model Evaluation and Validation Techniques are crucial aspects of the machine learning and statistical modeling process. Model evaluation and validation involve assessing the performance of a model and ensuring its generalization to unseen data. These techniques help identify the best models, fine-tune their parameters, and avoid overfitting, thus leading to better predictions and more accurate insights.

The need for model evaluation and validation arises from the inherent complexity and uncertainty in real-world data. Given a dataset, multiple models may capture the underlying relationships in the data to varying degrees of success. Therefore, it is essential to evaluate and compare different models to choose the one that performs the best on unseen data. Several model evaluation and validation techniques are used to assess model performance and ensure that they generalize well to new data.

Common Evaluation Techniques

Some popular techniques include:

- **Train-test split**: This technique involves dividing the dataset into training and test sets. The model is trained on the training set and its performance is evaluated on the test set. This approach helps assess the model's ability to generalize to unseen data.
- **Cross-validation**: Cross-validation is an extension of the train-test split method, where the dataset is divided into 'k' equally-sized partitions or "folds." The model is trained and tested 'k' times, each time using a different fold as the test set and the remaining folds as the training set. The average performance across all 'k' iterations is used to evaluate the

model. Cross-validation helps to mitigate the risk of overfitting and provides a more robust estimate of model performance.

- **Metrics**: Various metrics are used to measure model performance, depending on the task (e.g., classification, regression, clustering). For classification tasks, metrics such as accuracy, precision, recall, F1-score, and area under the ROC curve (AUC-ROC) are commonly used. For regression tasks, metrics like mean squared error (MSE), mean absolute error (MAE), and R-squared are popular.
- **Confusion Matrix**: A confusion matrix is a table that shows the true positive (TP), true negative (TN), false positive (FP), and false negative (FN) predictions for a classification model. It helps visualize the performance of the model and identify areas for improvement.
- **Learning Curves**: Learning curves plot the model's performance on the training and validation sets as a function of the number of training samples or iterations. They can help diagnose issues like overfitting and underfitting and guide the selection of the optimal model complexity.
- **Hyperparameter tuning**: Models often have hyperparameters that control their complexity or learning process. Techniques like grid search, random search, and Bayesian optimization can be used to find the best set of hyperparameters for a given model, leading to improved performance.
- **Model selection**: Model selection techniques, such as Akaike Information Criterion (AIC), Bayesian Information Criterion (BIC), and cross-validated performance, help in comparing and choosing the best model among several competing models.

We will explore some of these techniques in detail, along with a practical demonstration of each of them in further sections.

Train-Test Split

Understanding Train-Test Split

Train-test split is a fundamental and efficient method used to assess the performance of a machine learning model. This technique revolves around partitioning the available dataset into two distinct sets: the training set and the test set. Generally, a larger portion of the dataset is allocated for training purposes (typically around 70-80%), while the remaining smaller portion is reserved for testing (usually about 20-30%). The primary objective of this method is to teach the model using the training set, which contains various features and associated target values. Once the model has been trained, its performance is then evaluated using the test set. The test set, containing previously unseen data, provides a means to measure how effectively the model can generalize and make accurate predictions on new, unexplored data points.

The train-test split technique is crucial in preventing overfitting, a common issue in machine learning where a model performs exceptionally well on the training data but fails to deliver satisfactory results when exposed to unseen data. By segregating the dataset into separate training and testing sets, it becomes possible to identify and mitigate overfitting early in the development process.

Implementing Train-Test Split

Let's demonstrate how to perform a train-test split. To begin with, we will use the following crates:

- **ndarray** for numerical arrays.
- **csv** for reading CSV files.
- **rand** for random number generation.

```
use ndarray::{Array2, ArrayView2, ArrayView1, Axis, s};
use ndarray_csv::Array2Reader;
use rand::seq::SliceRandom;
use rand::thread_rng;
use std::error::Error;
use std::fs::File;
use std::io::BufReader;
```

First, as usual load the dataset. Then, shuffle and split the dataset as shown below:

```
fn train_test_split(
    x: &Array2<f64>,
    y: &Array2<f64>,
    test_size: f64,
) -> (Array2<f64>, Array2<f64>, Array2<f64>, Array2<f64>) {
    let n_samples = x.nrows();
    let indices: Vec<usize> = (0..n_samples).collect();
    let mut rng = thread_rng();
    let mut shuffled_indices = indices.clone();
    shuffled_indices.shuffle(&mut rng);
```

```
    let test_size = (n_samples as f64 * test_size).round() as
usize;
    let train_size = n_samples - test_size;
    let train_indices = &shuffled_indices[..train_size];
    let test_indices = &shuffled_indices[train_size..];
    let x_train = x.select(Axis(0), train_indices);
    let y_train = y.select(Axis(0), train_indices);
    let x_test = x.select(Axis(0), test_indices);
    let y_test = y.select(Axis(0), test_indices);
    (x_train, y_train, x_test, y_test)
}
```

Now, here we use a simple linear regression model from the **linfa** crate.

```
use linfa::prelude::*;
use linfa_linear::LinearRegression;
fn main() -> Result<(), Box<dyn Error>> {
    let (x, y) = load_dataset()?;
    let (x_train, y_train, x_test, y_test) =
train_test_split(&x, &y, 0.2);
    // Convert to Dataset
    let train_dataset = Dataset::new(x_train.clone(),
y_train.clone().column(0).to_owned());
    let test_dataset = Dataset::new(x_test.clone(),
y_test.clone().column(0).to_owned());
    // Train the model
    let model = LinearRegression::new().fit(&train_dataset)?;
    // Predict on test data
    let y_pred = model.predict(&test_dataset);
    // Evaluate the model
    let mse = y_pred.mean_squared_error(&test_dataset)?;
```

```
    println!("Mean Squared Error: {}", mse);
    Ok(())
}
```

To interpret the result, we will get the MSE, measuring the average squared difference between predicted and actual values. A lower MSE indicates better performance.

Cross-Validation Technique

Understanding Cross-Validation

Cross-validation represents a more sophisticated technique for evaluating models in comparison to the train-test split method. This approach is especially valuable when working with limited data since it utilizes the entire dataset for both training and testing purposes, thus mitigating the risk of overfitting. Among the various cross-validation strategies, **K-fold cross-validation** is widely recognized and employed.

The K-fold cross-validation method involves partitioning the dataset into K equally sized segments, referred to as folds. The model undergoes training and evaluation K times, with each iteration using a unique fold as the testing set and the remaining K-1 folds as the training set. This process ensures that every data point has the opportunity to be part of the test set, enhancing the reliability of the model evaluation. Once all iterations are complete, the final performance metric is derived by calculating the average of the performance metrics obtained during each individual iteration. This aggregated result offers a more comprehensive and accurate understanding of the model's performance, contributing to the development of more robust and reliable machine learning models that are better equipped to handle real-world scenarios.

Implementing K-Fold Cross-Validation

We will use the same dataset and also the same linear regression model. And, we will use **linfa**'s cross-validation capabilities.

```
use linfa::dataset::Dataset;
use linfa::metrics::Regression;
use linfa::prelude::*;
use linfa_linear::LinearRegression;
use ndarray::Array2;
use std::error::Error;
```

Next, we perform K-Fold Cross-Validation:

```
fn main() -> Result<(), Box<dyn Error>> {
    let (x, y) = load_dataset()?;
    let dataset = Dataset::new(x, y.column(0).to_owned());
    let n_splits = 5; // 5-fold cross-validation
    let mut mse_scores = Vec::new();
    for (train, valid) in dataset.iter_fold(n_splits) {
        let model = LinearRegression::new().fit(&train)?;
        let y_pred = model.predict(&valid);
        let mse = y_pred.mean_squared_error(&valid)?;
        mse_scores.push(mse);
    }
    let avg_mse = mse_scores.iter().sum::<f64>() /
mse_scores.len() as f64;
    println!("Average Mean Squared Error: {}", avg_mse);
    Ok(())
}
```

The result you get, includes:

- **Average MSE**: Provides a more reliable estimate of the model's performance.
- **Variance**: Analyze the variance of MSE scores to assess stability.

Hyperparameter Tuning

Understanding Hyperparameter Tuning

Hyperparameter tuning is the crucial process of optimizing a model's hyperparameters to achieve enhanced performance. Hyperparameters, unlike other parameters, are not learned from the data; rather, they are predetermined by the model's creator before the training process begins. Examples of hyperparameters include learning rates, regularization parameters, and the number of hidden layers in a neural network.

To provide a comprehensive understanding of hyperparameter tuning, let's delve into the most prevalent methods employed in this process:

- **Grid search**: The grid search method involves defining a range of potential values for each hyperparameter and then systematically testing every possible combination. While effective, this technique can be computationally demanding, particularly for models with an extensive set of hyperparameters.
- **Random search**: As an alternative to the exhaustive approach taken by grid search, random search selects and evaluates a random assortment of hyperparameter combinations. This technique frequently uncovers suitable hyperparameter values more rapidly than grid search, offering a more efficient solution.
- **Bayesian optimization**: This advanced method entails constructing a probabilistic model that captures the relationship between hyperparameters and overall model performance. Through iterative updates to this model, Bayesian optimization intelligently explores the hyperparameter space and swiftly converges to an optimal solution.

Each of these hyperparameter tuning methods has its advantages and drawbacks. Grid search offers a thorough exploration of the hyperparameter space but can be resource-intensive. Random search, while faster, may not be as exhaustive in its search for optimal hyperparameters. Bayesian optimization strikes a balance between the two, offering an intelligent and efficient approach to finding the best hyperparameters.

Implementing Grid Search

Let's perform hyperparameter tuning using Grid Search method for a Random Forest model using the **smartcore** crate.

After getting the libraries loaded, we define the hyperparameter grid:

```
let n_estimators_options = vec![50, 100, 150];
let max_depth_options = vec![None, Some(5), Some(10)];
let min_samples_split_options = vec![2, 5, 10];
```

Next, we implement grid search:

```
fn main() -> Result<(), Box<dyn Error>> {
    let (x, y) = load_dataset()?; // Use DenseMatrix for
smartcore
    let (x_train, y_train, x_test, y_test) =
train_test_split(&x, &y, 0.2);
    let mut best_params = None;
    let mut best_mse = f64::INFINITY;
```

```
    for &n_estimators in &n_estimators_options {
        for &max_depth in &max_depth_options {
            for &min_samples_split in
&min_samples_split_options {
                let params =
RandomForestRegressorParameters::default()
                    .with_n_estimators(n_estimators)
                    .with_max_depth(max_depth)

.with_min_samples_split(min_samples_split);
                let model =
RandomForestRegressor::fit(&x_train,
&y_train.column(0).to_vec(), params.clone())?;
                let y_pred = model.predict(&x_test)?;
                let mse =
mean_squared_error(&y_test.column(0).to_vec(), &y_pred);
                if mse < best_mse {
                    best_mse = mse;
                    best_params = Some(params);
                }
            }
        }
    }
    println!("Best MSE: {}", best_mse);
    println!("Best Parameters: {:?}", best_params);
    Ok(())
}
```

Now, we define mean squared error function:

```
fn mean_squared_error(y_true: &Vec<f64>, y_pred: &Vec<f64>) ->
f64 {
    y_true.iter()
```

```
        .zip(y_pred.iter())
        .map(|(a, b)| (a - b).powi(2))
        .sum::<f64>() / y_true.len() as f64
}
```

While interpreting the results, consider the following:

- **Best Parameters**: The combination of hyperparameters that resulted in the lowest MSE.
- **Model Performance**: Compare with default parameters to see the improvement.

Model Selection Techniques

Understanding AIC and BIC

The Akaike Information Criterion (AIC) and Bayesian Information Criterion (BIC) are powerful model selection techniques that assist in determining the optimal model among a range of candidate models. Both criteria emphasize the balance between goodness-of-fit and model complexity to ensure the most suitable model is chosen for a given dataset.

Akaike Information Criterion (AIC)

AIC, or Akaike Information Criterion, is a model selection metric that evaluates a model's goodness-of-fit while considering the number of parameters involved. A lower AIC value signifies a better-fitting model.

The formula for AIC is as follows:

AIC = $2k - 2ln(L)$

In this equation, 'k' represents the total number of model parameters, and 'L' denotes the maximized likelihood of the model given the data.

Bayesian Information Criterion (BIC)

BIC, or Bayesian Information Criterion, is another model selection metric that assesses the goodness-of-fit of a model while incorporating a penalty for model complexity. Similar to AIC, a lower BIC value corresponds to a better-fitting model.

The formula for BIC is as follows:

BIC = $k * ln(n) - 2ln(L)$

In this equation, 'k' stands for the total number of model parameters, 'n' represents the number of observations, and 'L' refers to the maximized likelihood of the model given the data.

Although AIC and BIC share conceptual similarities, BIC generally imposes a more significant penalty on model complexity than AIC. Consequently, BIC tends to favor simpler models in comparison to AIC. Both AIC and BIC are valuable tools in model selection, with each criterion focusing on achieving an optimal balance between goodness-of-fit and model complexity. By taking into account the number of parameters and the maximized likelihood of the model given the data, these criteria help researchers and data analysts identify the most suitable model for a particular dataset. While AIC and BIC share some similarities, the heavier penalty imposed on model complexity by BIC often results in the selection of simpler models compared to AIC. Ultimately, the choice between AIC and BIC depends on the specific context and goals of the analysis, as well as the preferences of the researcher or analyst involved.

Implementing AIC and BIC

Now, we will implement both, AIC and BIC for linear regression models with different features.

Define Models with Different Features

Suppose we have two models:

- Model 1: Uses features [work_year, experience_level].
- Model 2: Uses features [work_year, experience_level, remote_ratio].

Compute Log-Likelihood

For linear regression, the log-likelihood can be computed as:

$$ln(L) = -n2ln(2\pi\sigma 2) - 12\sigma 2\sum i = 1n(yi - y\hat{}i)2\backslash ln(L)$$

Since $\sigma 2$ (variance) is unknown, we can use the residual sum of squares (RSS) to compute AIC and BIC up to a constant.

Implement AIC and BIC Calculations

```
fn calculate_aic(n: usize, rss: f64, k: usize) -> f64 {
    n as f64 * (rss / n as f64).ln() + 2.0 * k as f64
}
fn calculate_bic(n: usize, rss: f64, k: usize) -> f64 {
    n as f64 * (rss / n as f64).ln() + (k as f64) * (n as
f64).ln()
}
```

Evaluate Models

```
fn main() -> Result<(), Box<dyn Error>> {
    let (x, y) = load_dataset()?;
    let n_samples = x.nrows();
    // Model 1
    let x1 = x.slice(s![.., 0..2]).to_owned(); // [work_year,
experience_level]
    let dataset1 = Dataset::new(x1, y.column(0).to_owned());
    let model1 = LinearRegression::new().fit(&dataset1)?;
    let y_pred1 = model1.predict(&dataset1);
    let rss1 = y_pred1.mean_squared_error(&dataset1)? *
n_samples as f64;
    let k1 = 2 + 1; // 2 features + intercept
    let aic1 = calculate_aic(n_samples, rss1, k1);
    let bic1 = calculate_bic(n_samples, rss1, k1);
    // Model 2
    let x2 = x.clone(); // [work_year, experience_level,
remote_ratio]
    let dataset2 = Dataset::new(x2, y.column(0).to_owned());
    let model2 = LinearRegression::new().fit(&dataset2)?;
    let y_pred2 = model2.predict(&dataset2);
    let rss2 = y_pred2.mean_squared_error(&dataset2)? *
n_samples as f64;
    let k2 = 3 + 1; // 3 features + intercept
    let aic2 = calculate_aic(n_samples, rss2, k2);
    let bic2 = calculate_bic(n_samples, rss2, k2);
    println!("Model 1 AIC: {}, BIC: {}", aic1, bic1);
    println!("Model 2 AIC: {}, BIC: {}", aic2, bic2);
    Ok(())
}
```

Finally, to interpret the results:

- **Compare AIC and BIC**: Lower values indicate a better model.
- **Model Selection**: Choose the model with the lower AIC/BIC.

Resampling Methods

Understanding Resampling Methods

Resampling methods constitute a set of statistical techniques that play a crucial role in model evaluation, hypothesis testing, and estimation of uncertainties inherent in data. These methods revolve around the core concept of recurrently sampling from the available data and recalculating relevant statistics. This process allows researchers and analysts to gain insights into the variability of the statistics, or to estimate their underlying distribution, thus enhancing the robustness of their conclusions.

Two prevalent types of resampling methods that have gained considerable traction in the field of statistics are **bootstrapping** and **permutation tests**.

Bootstrapping

Bootstrapping is a resampling method used to estimate the sampling distribution of a statistic by repeatedly drawing samples (with replacement) from the original dataset. It is particularly useful when the underlying distribution of the data is unknown or when the sample size is small. Bootstrapping can be applied to estimate confidence intervals, test hypotheses, and evaluate the stability of model parameters.

In a bootstrap procedure, you:

- Draw a random sample (with replacement) of the same size as the original dataset.
- Compute the statistic of interest from the resampled data.
- Repeat the both previous steps a large number of times (e.g., 1,000 or 10,000) to generate a distribution of the statistic.
- Estimate the sampling distribution of the statistic, such as calculating confidence intervals or standard errors.

Permutation Tests

Permutation tests, also known as randomization tests or exact tests, are non-parametric resampling methods used for hypothesis testing. They involve rearranging the observed data to create all possible permutations of the data (or a large random subset of permutations), and then calculating the test statistic for each permutation. By comparing the observed test statistic to the distribution of permuted test statistics, you can calculate a p-value to test the null hypothesis.

In a permutation test, you:

- Calculate the observed test statistic for the original data.
- Randomly permute the data (or a subset of the data) and calculate the test statistic for the permuted data.
- Repeat the previous step a large number of times (e.g., 1,000 or 10,000) to generate a distribution of permuted test statistics.
- Calculate the p-value as the proportion of permuted test statistics that are as extreme or more extreme than the observed test statistic.

Both, bootstrapping and permutation tests offer flexible and powerful methods for statistical inference, as they do not rely on strong assumptions about the underlying data distribution. They can be applied to a wide range of problems and are particularly useful when working with small sample sizes or non-normally distributed data.

Implementing Bootstrapping and Permutation Tests

Let's estimate the confidence interval for the mean salary and test if there's a significant difference between salaries of two job titles.

To begin with, first load and split the data into groups:

```
fn load_salary_by_job_title(job_title: &str) ->
Result<Vec<f64>, Box<dyn Error>> {

    let file = File::open("ds_salaries.csv")?;

    let mut rdr =
csv::Reader::from_reader(BufReader::new(file));

    let mut salaries = Vec::new();

    for result in rdr.records() {

        let record = result?;

        if record.get(3).unwrap() == job_title {

            let salary_in_usd: f64 =
record.get(4).unwrap().parse()?;

            salaries.push(salary_in_usd);

        }

    }
```

```
    Ok(salaries)
}
```

Now, start performing bootstrapping:

```
fn bootstrap_mean(salaries: &Vec<f64>, n_bootstrap: usize) ->
Vec<f64> {
    let mut rng = thread_rng();
    let mut bootstrap_means = Vec::with_capacity(n_bootstrap);
    for _ in 0..n_bootstrap {
        let sample: Vec<f64> = salaries
            .choose_multiple(&mut rng, salaries.len())
            .cloned()
            .collect();
        let mean = sample.iter().sum::<f64>() / sample.len()
as f64;
        bootstrap_means.push(mean);
    }
    bootstrap_means
}
```

We then calculate confidence intervals:

```
fn confidence_interval(data: &mut Vec<f64>, percentile: f64) -
> (f64, f64) {
    data.sort_by(|a, b| a.partial_cmp(b).unwrap());
    let lower_idx = ((1.0 - percentile) / 2.0 * data.len() as
f64) as usize;
    let upper_idx = ((1.0 + percentile) / 2.0 * data.len() as
f64) as usize;
    (data[lower_idx], data[upper_idx])
}
```

Now, perform permutation test:

```
fn permutation_test(
    group1: &Vec<f64>,
    group2: &Vec<f64>,
    n_permutations: usize,
) -> f64 {
    let observed_diff = group1.iter().sum::<f64>() /
group1.len() as f64
        - group2.iter().sum::<f64>() / group2.len() as f64;
    let mut combined = [group1.clone(),
group2.clone()].concat();
    let mut rng = thread_rng();
    let mut count = 0;
    for _ in 0..n_permutations {
        combined.shuffle(&mut rng);
        let permuted_group1 = &combined[..group1.len()];
        let permuted_group2 = &combined[group1.len()..];
        let permuted_diff =
permuted_group1.iter().sum::<f64>() / permuted_group1.len() as
f64
            - permuted_group2.iter().sum::<f64>() /
permuted_group2.len() as f64;
        if permuted_diff.abs() >= observed_diff.abs() {
            count += 1;
        }
    }
    count as f64 / n_permutations as f64
}
```

Then, you can run the analysis:

```
fn main() -> Result<(), Box<dyn Error>> {
```

```
    let salaries1 = load_salary_by_job_title("Data
Scientist")?;
    let salaries2 = load_salary_by_job_title("Data
Engineer")?;
    // Bootstrapping
    let n_bootstrap = 1000;
    let mut bootstrap_means1 = bootstrap_mean(&salaries1,
n_bootstrap);
    let mut bootstrap_means2 = bootstrap_mean(&salaries2,
n_bootstrap);
    let ci1 = confidence_interval(&mut bootstrap_means1,
0.95);
    let ci2 = confidence_interval(&mut bootstrap_means2,
0.95);
    println!("Data Scientist mean salary 95% CI: {:?}", ci1);
    println!("Data Engineer mean salary 95% CI: {:?}", ci2);
    // Permutation Test
    let n_permutations = 1000;
    let p_value = permutation_test(&salaries1, &salaries2,
n_permutations);
    println!("Permutation test p-value: {}", p_value);
    Ok(())
}
```

While interpreting the results, consider:

- **Confidence Intervals**: Provide a range within which the true mean salary likely falls.
- **Permutation Test p-value**: A small p-value (e.g., < 0.05) indicates a significant difference between the groups.

Summary

As a result of finishing this chapter, you have improved your capacity to evaluate and validate models in an efficient manner. You used evaluation techniques like cross-validation and hyperparameter tuning to ensure that your models perform well on unseen data. You recognized the importance of using appropriate metrics and avoiding overfitting.

You also explored model selection criteria such as AIC and BIC, which allowed you to select models that balanced complexity and performance. You gained insights into your models' variability and reliability by using resampling techniques. In professional data analysis, these skills are required to create accurate and trustworthy models.

CHAPTER 11: TEXT AND NATURAL LANGUAGE PROCESSING

Introduction

You have reached the final chapter of this book, and in this chapter, you will explore natural language processing (NLP) and text processing. You are going to acquire the knowledge necessary to preprocess text data, which includes stemming, tokenization, and the removal of stopwords. You will be able to effectively manage unstructured data by preparing text for analysis with the help of Rust's regex, unicode-segmentation, and rust-stemmers crates.

In this chapter, advanced natural language processing techniques such as TF-IDF for information retrieval and Word2Vec for word embeddings are explored. You are going to implement these methods to extract meaningful information from textual data. You will be able to tackle natural language processing tasks by the time you reach the end of this chapter, which will open up new avenues for data analysis.

Overview of Natural Language Processing

Natural Language Processing (NLP) is a subfield of artificial intelligence (AI) and linguistics that focuses on enabling computers to understand, interpret, and generate human language in a valuable way. The goal of NLP is to bridge the gap between human communication and computer understanding, allowing for more natural interactions between humans and machines. Over the past several decades, NLP has evolved significantly, driven by advancements in computational power, the availability of large datasets, and the development of sophisticated algorithms.

Historical Development of NLP

The development of NLP began in the 1950s with the advent of computational linguistics. One of the earliest milestones was the **Georgetown-IBM experiment** in 1954, where a machine translation system translated over 60 Russian sentences into English. This demonstrated the potential for machines to process human language.

In the 1960s and 1970s, research shifted towards **rule-based systems**. Linguists like **Noam Chomsky** introduced formal grammars, laying the groundwork for syntactic parsing. Systems like **SHRDLU**, developed by Terry Winograd, could understand and execute commands within a restricted domain, showcasing early attempts at natural language understanding.

The 1980s marked the rise of **statistical methods** in NLP. Researchers began to leverage probabilistic models, such as **Hidden Markov Models (HMMs)**, for tasks like part-of-speech tagging and speech recognition. This shift was fueled by the availability of larger corpora and the realization that language could be modeled statistically.

The 1990s and early 2000s saw the emergence of **machine learning techniques** in NLP. Algorithms like **Support Vector Machines (SVMs)** and **Decision Trees** were applied to NLP tasks, leading to improvements in areas like text classification and sentiment analysis. The explosion of the internet provided vast amounts of textual data, further propelling NLP research.

A significant breakthrough came in 2013 with the introduction of **Word2Vec** by Mikolov et al., which used neural networks to generate word embeddings, capturing semantic relationships between words in vector space. This was followed by models like **GloVe** and **fastText**, which further refined word embeddings.

The introduction of the **Transformer architecture** by Vaswani et al. in 2017 revolutionized NLP. Transformers enabled models to capture long-range dependencies in text more effectively. Building on this, large-scale pre-trained models like **BERT** (Bidirectional Encoder Representations from Transformers) and **GPT** (Generative Pre-trained Transformer) demonstrated unprecedented performance across a wide range of NLP tasks.

Adoption and Applications of NLP

Today, NLP is ubiquitous, powering applications we interact with daily:

- **Search Engines**: Understanding queries and retrieving relevant information.
- **Virtual Assistants**: Siri, Alexa, and Google Assistant rely on NLP to understand voice commands.
- **Machine Translation**: Services like Google Translate break language barriers.
- **Sentiment Analysis**: Businesses analyze customer feedback on social media.
- **Chatbots**: Automated customer service agents handle routine inquiries.
- **Text Summarization**: Condensing large documents into concise summaries.
- **Spam Detection**: Filtering unwanted emails.

The evolution of NLP continues as models become more sophisticated, datasets grow larger, and computational resources become more powerful.

Key Processes in Natural Language Processing

To effectively process and understand human language, NLP relies on a series of key processes that transform raw text into structured data that machines can interpret.

Tokenization

One of the essential processes in NLP is tokenization. Tokenization involves breaking down text into individual words or tokens, which is crucial as it allows NLP systems to analyze text at the word level. By analyzing words individually, NLP algorithms can identify patterns and relationships between words and phrases, which is useful for tasks such as sentiment analysis and named entity recognition.

For example:

```
Input: "Natural Language Processing is fascinating."
Tokens: ["Natural", "Language", "Processing", "is",
"fascinating", "."]
```

Stopword Removal

Another important process in NLP is stopword removal. Stopwords are common words that do not carry much meaning in the context of text analysis, such as "the," "and," and "is." Removing stopwords can help reduce the dimensionality of the data, making it easier for NLP algorithms to analyze and process text.

For example:

```
Input Tokens: ["Natural", "Language", "Processing", "is",
"fascinating", "."]
Stopwords: ["is", "."]
After Removal: ["Natural", "Language", "Processing",
"fascinating"]
```

Stemming and Lemmatization

Stemming and lemmatization are also key processes in NLP. Both processes aim to reduce words to their base or root form, which can help consolidate similar words and reduce noise in the text data. Stemming is a crude process that removes affixes from words, while lemmatization is more sophisticated, taking into account the morphological structure and context of the word.

For example:

"Running" → "Run"

"Studies" → "Studi"

"Running" → "Run" (lemmatization)

"Better" → "Good" (lemmatization)

Lemmatization is generally more accurate but requires more computational resources.

Part-of-Speech (POS) Tagging

POS tagging involves labeling each token with its grammatical role, such as noun, verb, adjective, etc. This provides syntactic context, which is essential for understanding the structure and meaning of sentences.

For example:

```
Sentence: "The quick brown fox jumps over the lazy dog."
POS Tags: [("The", "DT"), ("quick", "JJ"), ("brown", "JJ"),
("fox", "NN"), ("jumps", "VBZ"), ("over", "IN"), ("the",
"DT"), ("lazy", "JJ"), ("dog", "NN")]
```

Named Entity Recognition (NER)

Named Entity Recognition (NER) is the process of identifying and classifying named entities, such as people, organizations, and locations, in the text. NER can be useful for extracting structured information from unstructured text data, such as customer feedback or social media posts.

For example:

```
Sentence: "Apple Inc. was founded by Steve Jobs."
Entities: [("Apple Inc.", "Organization"), ("Steve Jobs",
"Person")]
```

Dependency Parsing

Dependency parsing is another important process in NLP that involves analyzing the grammatical structure of a sentence to identify the relationships between words. By identifying the relationships between words, NLP algorithms can understand the semantic meaning of sentences and identify complex relationships in the text.

For example:

```
Sentence: "She enjoys playing tennis."
Dependencies:
- "enjoys" is the root verb.
- "She" is the subject of "enjoys".
- "playing" is a direct object of "enjoys".
- "tennis" is the object of "playing".
```

Sentiment Analysis

Sentiment analysis is a process that aims to determine the sentiment or emotion expressed in a piece of text. Sentiment analysis can be useful for understanding public opinion, customer feedback, and social media trends.

For example:

```
Text: "I love this new phone; it's fantastic!"
Sentiment: Positive
```

Machine Translation

Machine translation is a process that focuses on automatically translating text from one language to another. Recent advancements in neural machine translation have greatly improved the quality and efficiency of this process, making it possible for people to communicate with others who speak different languages.

For example:

```
Input: "Bonjour tout le monde."
Output: "Hello everyone."
```

Text Summarization

Text summarization creates a condensed version of a text that retains the main points. It can be:

- **Extractive**: Selecting important sentences from the original text.
- **Abstractive**: Generating new sentences that capture the essence of the text.

These key NLP processes let machines understand and process language, doing things that were impossible before. By breaking text into words, removing unnecessary words, and reducing words to their root form, NLP algorithms can analyze text at the word level, identify patterns and relationships between words, and understand the meaning of sentences. The different processes and techniques involved in NLP have made it possible to analyze, interpret, and generate human language effectively, which has led to lots of applications that have transformed the way we interact with technology and access information.

Text Preprocessing and Tokenization

Text preprocessing and tokenization are two essential tasks in natural language processing (NLP) that are performed on raw textual data before further analysis or processing. Text preprocessing involves cleaning and transforming the raw data to make it suitable for analysis. Tokenization is the process of breaking down the text into smaller meaningful units called tokens.

Key Preprocessing Techniques

Some common text preprocessing techniques include:

- Lowercasing: Converting all text to lowercase can help establish uniformity and make it easier to match tokens, as algorithms are usually case-sensitive.
- Removing punctuation, special characters, and numbers: These elements can introduce noise and are often unnecessary for text analysis. By removing them, you can reduce the complexity of the text.
- Removing stopwords: Stopwords are common words like 'the,' 'is,' and 'in,' which don't carry much meaning and can be removed to reduce the dimensionality of the text data.
- Stemming and Lemmatization: These techniques reduce words to their base or root form. Stemming involves truncating words, while lemmatization uses a linguistic approach to convert words to their base form. Both techniques help in grouping similar words together.

Tokenization Approaches

After preprocessing the text, tokenization can be performed using several approaches:

- Word tokenization: In this method, the text is split into individual words based on spaces or punctuation marks.
- Sentence tokenization: The text is split into sentences, usually based on punctuation marks like periods, question marks, or exclamation marks.
- Subword tokenization: This approach breaks text down into smaller units like syllables, characters, or morphemes. It's particularly useful for languages where word boundaries are not easily identifiable, or for tasks that require a more granular understanding of the text.

Implementing Text Preprocessing and Tokenization

We will work with a sample dataset containing over 200,000 text messages, available at the following URL:

https://raw.githubusercontent.com/kittenpub/database-repository/main/200000_noemoticon_nlp_data.csv

You'll need to import some libraries as shown below:

```
use csv::Reader;

use reqwest::blocking::get;

use std::error::Error;

use unicode_segmentation::UnicodeSegmentation; // For
tokenization
```

```
use regex::Regex; // For preprocessing
```

Then, load the data:

```
fn load_data(url: &str) -> Result<Vec<String>, Box<dyn Error>>
{
    let mut data = Vec::new();
    let response = get(url)?.text()?;
    let mut reader = Reader::from_reader(response.as_bytes());
    for result in reader.records() {
        let record = result?;
        // Assuming the text is in the 6th column (index 5)
        data.push(record[5].to_string());
    }
    Ok(data)
}
```

Next, preprocess the text:

```
fn preprocess_text(text: &str) -> String {
    // Convert to lowercase
    let text = text.to_lowercase();
    // Remove URLs
    let url_re = Regex::new(r"http\S+").unwrap();
    let text = url_re.replace_all(&text, "");
    // Remove non-alphanumeric characters (excluding spaces)
    let non_alpha_num_re = Regex::new(r"[^a-zA-Z0-
9\s]").unwrap();
    let text = non_alpha_num_re.replace_all(&text, "");
    // Remove extra whitespaces
    let text =
text.split_whitespace().collect::<Vec<&str>>().join(" ");
    text
```

```
}
```

Now, tokenize the text:

```
fn tokenize(text: &str) -> Vec<String> {
    text.unicode_words().map(|s| s.to_string()).collect()
}
```

Following is the sample output:

```
Original text: @switchfoot http://twitpic.com/2y1zl - Awww,
that's a bummer.  You shoulda got David Carr of Third Day to
do it. ;D

Tokens: ["switchfoot", "awww", "thats", "a", "bummer", "you",
"shoulda", "got", "david", "carr", "of", "third", "day", "to",
"do", "it", "d"]

Original text: is upset that he can't update his Facebook by
texting it... and might cry as a result  School today also.
Blah!

Tokens: ["is", "upset", "that", "he", "cant", "update", "his",
"facebook", "by", "texting", "it", "and", "might", "cry",
"as", "a", "result", "school", "today", "also", "blah"]

Original text: @Kenichan I dived many times for the ball.
Managed to save 50%  The rest go out of bounds

Tokens: ["kenichan", "i", "dived", "many", "times", "for",
"the", "ball", "managed", "to", "save", "50", "the", "rest",
"go", "out", "of", "bounds"]
```

Implement Stopword Removal

Stopword removal is the process of eliminating common words that don't carry much meaning and are often found in large quantities in text data. Examples of stopwords include "the," "is," "in," "and," etc. Removing stopwords can help reduce the dimensionality of the text data and improve the performance of text processing algorithms.

To begin with, first create a stopword list. You can also use a predefined list or create a custom one.

```
use std::collections::HashSet;

fn get_stopwords() -> HashSet<String> {
    let stopwords = [
        "a", "an", "and", "are", "as", "at", "be", "by",
"for", "from", "has", "he", "in", "is",
        "it", "its", "of", "on", "that", "the", "to", "was",
"were", "will", "with", "i", "you",
        "she", "they", "we", "this", "there", "their",
    ];
    stopwords.iter().map(|s| s.to_string()).collect()
}
```

Next, remove stopwords from tokens:

```
fn remove_stopwords(tokens: Vec<String>, stopwords:
&HashSet<String>) -> Vec<String> {
    tokens
        .into_iter()
        .filter(|token| !stopwords.contains(token))
        .collect()
}
```

Next, update the program:

```
fn main() -> Result<(), Box<dyn Error>> {
    let url =
"https://raw.githubusercontent.com/kittenpub/database-
repository/main/200000_noemoticon_nlp_data.csv";
    let data = load_data(url)?;
    let stopwords = get_stopwords();
    // Process and tokenize the first 5 records
    for text in data.iter().take(5) {
        let preprocessed_text = preprocess_text(text);
```

```
        let tokens = tokenize(&preprocessed_text);
        let filtered_tokens = remove_stopwords(tokens,
&stopwords);
        println!("Original text: {}", text);
        println!("Tokens without stopwords: {:?}",
filtered_tokens);
        println!();
    }
    Ok(())
}
```

Following is the sample output:

```
Original text: @switchfoot http://twitpic.com/2y1zl - Awww,
that's a bummer.  You shoulda got David Carr of Third Day to
do it. ;D
Tokens without stopwords: ["switchfoot", "awww", "thats",
"bummer", "shoulda", "got", "david", "carr", "third", "day",
"do", "d"]
Original text: is upset that he can't update his Facebook by
texting it... and might cry as a result  School today also.
Blah!
Tokens without stopwords: ["upset", "cant", "update",
"facebook", "texting", "might", "cry", "result", "school",
"today", "also", "blah"]
Original text: @Kenichan I dived many times for the ball.
Managed to save 50%  The rest go out of bounds
Tokens without stopwords: ["kenichan", "dived", "many",
"times", "ball", "managed", "save", "50", "rest", "go", "out",
"bounds"]
```

Stemming and Lemmatization

Understanding Stemming and Lemmatization

Stemming and lemmatization are techniques used in natural language processing to simplify words down to their root or base forms. By reducing variations of the same word, this can make it easier to analyze text more effectively. Stemming is a simpler technique that just trims off the ends of words, while lemmatization is a more sophisticated process that considers the context and part of speech to derive the fundamental form of a word.

As of now, there isn't a quick and easy way to get this done in Rust. Rust doesn't have a built-in tool that's as good as NLTK or SpaCy for stemming and lemmatization, but it does have the rust_stemmers library for stemming, so that's worth looking into.

Implementing Stemming

To begin with, first add dependency to Cargo.toml:

```
[dependencies]
rust-stemmers = "1.2.0"
```

Next, import and use the stemmer:

```
use rust_stemmers::{Algorithm, Stemmer};
fn stem_tokens(tokens: Vec<String>) -> Vec<String> {
    let stemmer = Stemmer::create(Algorithm::English);
    tokens
        .into_iter()
        .map(|token| stemmer.stem(&token).to_string())
        .collect()
}
```

Now, update the program:

```
fn main() -> Result<(), Box<dyn Error>> {
    let url =
"https://raw.githubusercontent.com/kittenpub/database-
repository/main/200000_noemoticon_nlp_data.csv";
    let data = load_data(url)?;
    let stopwords = get_stopwords();
    // Process and tokenize the first 5 records
    for text in data.iter().take(5) {
```

```
        let preprocessed_text = preprocess_text(text);
        let tokens = tokenize(&preprocessed_text);
        let filtered_tokens = remove_stopwords(tokens,
&stopwords);
        let stemmed_tokens = stem_tokens(filtered_tokens);
        println!("Original text: {}", text);
        println!("Stemmed tokens: {:?}", stemmed_tokens);
        println!();
    }
    Ok(())
}
```

Following is the possible output:

```
Original text: @switchfoot http://twitpic.com/2y1zl - Awww,
that's a bummer.  You shoulda got David Carr of Third Day to
do it. ;D
Stemmed tokens: ["switchfoot", "awww", "that", "bummer",
"shoulda", "got", "david", "carr", "third", "day", "do", "d"]
Original text: is upset that he can't update his Facebook by
texting it... and might cry as a result  School today also.
Blah!
Stemmed tokens: ["upset", "cant", "updat", "facebook", "text",
"might", "cri", "result", "school", "today", "also", "blah"]
Original text: @Kenichan I dived many times for the ball.
Managed to save 50%  The rest go out of bounds
Stemmed tokens: ["kenichan", "dive", "mani", "time", "ball",
"manag", "save", "50", "rest", "go", "out", "bound"]
```

Information Retrieval with TF-IDF

Understanding TF-IDF

TF-IDF, which stands for Term Frequency-Inverse Document Frequency, is a numerical statistic used in natural language processing and information retrieval. It is a technique that assigns a weight to each word in a document, based on its importance in the document and within the entire corpus. The importance of a word increases with its frequency in a document but is offset by its frequency across all documents.

TF-IDF has two components:

- Term Frequency (TF): This measures the frequency of a word in a document. It can be calculated as the number of times a word appears in a document divided by the total number of words in the document.
- Inverse Document Frequency (IDF): This measures the importance of a word across the entire corpus. It can be calculated as the logarithm of the total number of documents divided by the number of documents containing the word.

The product of TF and IDF gives the TF-IDF score for each word in a document.

Implementing TF-IDF

Now, to implement TF-IDF, we'll process the dataset and compute the TF-IDF scores.

At first, create data structures:

```
use std::collections::HashMap;
```

Now, calculate term frequencies:

```
fn compute_tf(tokens: &[String]) -> HashMap<String, f64> {
    let mut tf_map = HashMap::new();
    let total_tokens = tokens.len() as f64;
    for token in tokens {
        *tf_map.entry(token.clone()).or_insert(0.0) += 1.0;
    }
    for value in tf_map.values_mut() {
        *value /= total_tokens;
    }
    tf_map
}
```

Next, calculate inverse document frequencies:

```
fn compute_idf(documents: &[Vec<String>]) -> HashMap<String,
f64> {
    let mut idf_map = HashMap::new();
    let total_documents = documents.len() as f64;
    for doc in documents {
        let unique_tokens: Vec<&String> =
doc.iter().collect();
        for token in unique_tokens {
            idf_map.entry(token.clone()).or_insert(0.0);
        }
    }
    for token in idf_map.keys() {
        let mut count = 0;
        for doc in documents {
            if doc.contains(token) {
                count += 1;
            }
        }
        idf_map.insert(token.clone(), (total_documents / (1.0
+ count as f64)).ln());
    }
    idf_map
}
```

Now, compute TF-IDF scores:

```
fn compute_tfidf(tf: &HashMap<String, f64>, idf:
&HashMap<String, f64>) -> HashMap<String, f64>
{
    let mut tfidf_map = HashMap::new();
    for (token, tf_value) in tf {
        if let Some(idf_value) = idf.get(token) {
```

```
            tfidf_map.insert(token.clone(), tf_value *
idf_value);
        }
    }
    tfidf_map
}
```

Then, simply update the program:

```
fn main() -> Result<(), Box<dyn Error>> {
    let url =
"https://raw.githubusercontent.com/kittenpub/database-
repository/main/200000_noemoticon_nlp_data.csv";
    let data = load_data(url)?;
    let stopwords = get_stopwords();
    // Process and tokenize documents
    let mut documents = Vec::new();
    for text in data.iter().take(1000) { // Limiting to 1000
documents for performance
        let preprocessed_text = preprocess_text(text);
        let tokens = tokenize(&preprocessed_text);
        let filtered_tokens = remove_stopwords(tokens,
&stopwords);
        let stemmed_tokens = stem_tokens(filtered_tokens);
        documents.push(stemmed_tokens);
    }
    // Compute IDF across all documents
    let idf = compute_idf(&documents);
    // Compute TF-IDF for the first document
    let doc_tokens = &documents[0];
    let tf = compute_tf(doc_tokens);
    let tfidf = compute_tfidf(&tf, &idf);
```

```
    // Print top 5 TF-IDF scores
    let mut tfidf_vec: Vec<(&String, &f64)> =
tfidf.iter().collect();
    tfidf_vec.sort_by(|a, b| b.1.partial_cmp(a.1).unwrap());
    println!("Top 5 TF-IDF scores for the first document:");
    for (token, score) in tfidf_vec.iter().take(5) {
        println!("{}: {:.5}", token, score);
    }
    Ok(())
}
```

Following will be the possible outcome:

```
Top 5 TF-IDF scores for the first document:
switchfoot: 0.00000
awww: 0.00000
bummer: 0.00000
shoulda: 0.00000
got: 0.00000
```

Now, remember that due to the small number of documents and the simplified implementation, the TF-IDF scores may not reflect meaningful values. In practice, a larger corpus and optimized calculations are necessary.

Word Embeddings and Word2Vec

Understanding Word Embeddings

Word embeddings are dense vector representations of words that capture their semantic meaning. They allow algorithms to work with text data by converting it into numerical format. One popular word embedding technique is Word2Vec, which generates embeddings by training a shallow neural network on a large corpus. We can use the finalfusion crate to read pre-trained word embeddings and use them in your Rust project.

Implementing Word Embeddings

While training Word2Vec models from scratch requires significant resources, we can use pre-trained embeddings.

To begin with, first you'll need to add finalfusion to your Cargo.toml:

```
[dependencies]
finalfusion = "0.16.0"
```

Then, download embeddings in **finalfusion** format from Finalfusion Pretrained Vectors.

```
use finalfusion::prelude::*;
use std::fs::File;
use std::io::BufReader;
use std::error::Error;
fn main() -> Result<(), Box<dyn Error>> {
    let path = "embeddings/enwiki.fifu"; // Update with your
embeddings path
    let f = File::open(path)?;
    let mut reader = BufReader::new(f);
    let embeddings: Embeddings<VocabWrap, StorageWrap> =
Embeddings::read_embeddings(&mut reader)?;
    let word = "king";
    if let Some(embedding) = embeddings.embedding(word) {
        println!("Embedding for '{}': {:?}", word, embedding);
    } else {
        println!("Word '{}' not found in embeddings.", word);
    }
    Ok(())
}
```

Then, we can perform word analogies:

```
if let (Some(king), Some(man), Some(woman)) = (
    embeddings.embedding("king"),
    embeddings.embedding("man"),
```

```
    embeddings.embedding("woman"),
) {
    let queen = &king - &man + &woman;
    if let Some((similar_word, _)) =
embeddings.similarity(&queen).next() {
        println!("Analogy result: 'king' - 'man' + 'woman' =
'{}'", similar_word);
    }
}
```

Given below can be the right outcome of the above program:

```
Analogy result: 'king' - 'man' + 'woman' = 'queen'
```

This demonstrates how word embeddings capture semantic relationships.

Summary

As you finish this last chapter, you will have a solid grasp of Rust's fundamentals for text and NLP. The procedures of text preprocessing were carried out by you, and you prepared the raw text data for analysis. You improved your capacity to handle textual data in a programmatic manner by implementing stemming, tokenization, and the elimination of stopwords.

In addition to that, you worked with word embeddings and advanced natural language processing techniques, such as computing TF-IDF scores. You applied these techniques to text data in order to get insights. As a Rust specialist, these abilities expand your career prospects in areas such as language modeling, information retrieval, and sentiment analysis.

Index

a

b

c

d

e

f

g

h

i

k

l

m

n

o

p

q

r

Epilogue

As I wrap up this chapter of "Statistics with Rust, Second Edition," I'm flooded with a sense of relief and accomplishment! Writing this book has been an incredible journey! It's been both demanding and exhilarating, filled with late nights of coding, countless revisions, and moments of deep reflection. I'm thrilled to have brought together the worlds of statistics and Rust programming as a passion project, and seeing it come to fruition is incredibly fulfilling.

I've been on a mission to share not just knowledge but also the sheer excitement that comes with discovering new ways to solve problems throughout this process! Rust is an amazing partner for exploring statistical concepts! It's all about safety and performance, which makes it a perfect fit for this work. I've loved putting together examples that not only show how the theories work but also demonstrate how Rust can handle complex calculations really well.

There were times when I questioned whether certain ideas could be effectively translated into Rust, especially when dealing with advanced statistical methods or natural language processing tasks. But I was excited to find out if they could! But each challenge became an amazing opportunity to push boundaries and find innovative solutions! Collaborating with the vibrant Rust community and seeing the continual growth of its ecosystem gave me the encouragement I needed to keep moving forward. It's been so rewarding to integrate practical programs into the book! I believe that hands-on experience is invaluable, and I wanted to ensure that you, the reader, could actively engage with the material. It brings me immense joy to know that these programs might spark inspiration or help you overcome a hurdle in your own projects!

Now that I've finished this, I'm done. I've put my pen down (or, more accurately, closed my laptop), and I feel a weight lifted off my shoulders. My countless hours of writing, coding, and revising have culminated in something tangible that will undoubtedly make a positive impact. I am pleased to have successfully navigated the complexities and delivered a work that aligns with my original vision.

I am grateful to the colleagues, friends, and Rust community who offered insights and feedback along the way. Their encouragement made the challenging moments manageable and the successes even sweeter.

Thank You

www.ingramcontent.com/pod-product-compliance
Lightning Source LLC
Chambersburg PA
CBHW080212170726
48282CB00030B/1094
9788119177974